"The world was peopled
with wonders."

The origin of Wildsam comes from above, a
line of prose in the novel *East of Eden*, written by
John Steinbeck. Six words hinting at a broad and
interwoven idea. One of curiosity, connection, joy. And
the belief that stories have the power to unearth the
mysteries of a place—for anyone. The book in
your hands is rooted in such things.

Many thanks to the California Historical Society, San Francisco
History Center, GLBT Historical Society Museum, Heidi
Julavits at *The Believer*, Amanda Schoonmaker at Farrar, Straus
& Giroux. So many people have helped us understand and explore
San Francisco. Thanks to La Cocina, the Phoenix, Janet Ozzard,
Douglas McGray, Bart Sights, Ligaya Tichy, August Kleinzahler,
Julie Orringer, Chris Colin, Barrett Austin, Samantha Alviani,
Josh Baker, Michael Newhouse. Jennifer Maerz and Valerie
Luu shared hints on writers and dive bars, respectively; George
McCalman and Shelley Wong lent perspective and ideas as well
as their own wonderful words. In rough times and smooth,
San Francisco remains a beacon on our Western shore.

WILDSAM FIELD GUIDES™

Published in the United States
by Wildsam Field Guides, Austin, Texas.

ISBN 978-1-4671-9962-9

Illustrations by Lisa Congdon

To find more field guides, please visit
www.wildsam.com

CONTENTS

*Discover the people and places
that tell the story of San Francisco*

WELCOME

———

THE BREATH-STEALING VIEWS. Two-tone horns in the fog. A slice of warm Tartine bread.

San Francisco is a city for the senses. If you live here, you could name five hundred moments like these. Listen. Taste. Watch. The city flings moments at your feet like flowers. Not all cities do this, filling the memory banks with such generosity. San Francisco does it from the very beginning. Kerouac wrote, "Ahead of us the fabulous white city of San Francisco on her eleven mystic hills with the blue Pacific and its advancing wall of potato-patch fog beyond, and smoke and goldenness in the late afternoon of time." He felt the vim, the elevated life. The treble knob turned to newer, higher frequencies on this seven-mile peninsula.

From its very beginnings, San Francisco wore the mystical power of the West. That magnetic pull, capturing the zeitgeist—gold rush, Summer of Love, tech boom—and promising opportunities, ideas and new identities. It's the city where Jack London honed his storytelling, where Joe DiMaggio played high school ball, where Etta James found her voice. Where thousands of African Americans migrated during World War II, escaping Jim Crow for new lives on a new coast. Where runaways hitchhiked. Magnet for generations of Chinese families. In many ways, San Francisco is a global rallying point for dreamers, a fragrant city that the Spanish chose to name *Yerba Buena*, good herbs. One wonders if there's some magic, maybe a spell cast by space. And sea. The thousands of miles between *there* and *here*. Time given to shed old skins. To ditch the baggage and picture something new.

Rebecca Solnit writes that San Francisco is "where America comes to reinvent itself." It could be said just as well that the city is always somewhere in the midst of self-renewal. San Francisco rose again from earthquake ruins, and follows every bust with a boom. This all seems to have a mysterious logic of its own. No gold rush prosepctor would have predicted the hippies. No love-in held a specific clue to high tech. Somehow, here, it happened. This book is filled with such stories. San Francisco in every age is a five-sense city. It's fully alive, and it never rests. —The Editors

ESSENTIALS

TRANSPORT

CABLE CARS
SFMTA
Powell & Market

....

SAILBOATS
Spinnaker Sailing
spinnaker-sailing.com

LANDMARKS

COIT TOWER
1 *Telegraph Hill Blvd*
Art deco outpost, 1930s murals.

....

LOMBARD STREET
Russian Hill
Chase-scene gold, with 8
dramatic zigs and zags.

....

TONGA ROOM
950 *Mason St*
Hallucinatory nights since 1945.
All-out tropical decor, indoor
storms as live band swings.

MEDIA

PUBLIC RADIO
KQED
Forum call-in lets it all out.

....

REPORTING
Mission Local
Sharp neighborhood coverage.

....

LITERARY MAGAZINE
Zyzzyva
A-list stories, interviews.

GREENSPACE

GOLDEN GATE PARK
Great Highway
SF's crossroads, with Japanese
Tea Garden, tulips, lakes.

....

ALAMO SQUARE PARK
Hayes & Styner
A rustic rise for spying the
famed Painted Lady homes.

....

PRESIDIO GOLF COURSE
300 *Finley Rd*
A historic public course among
the eucalyptus.

CALENDAR

JAN - APR
Film Noir Festival
Chinese New Year Parade
Cherry Blossom Festival
MAY - JUL
Carnaval
Pride
Fillmore Jazz Fest
AUG - DEC
Folsom Street Fair
Día de los Muertos
Golden Gate Half Marathon

BOOKS

≥ *Infinite City*
  by Rebecca Solnit
≥ *The Dain Curse*
  by Dashiell Hammett
≥ *The Joy Luck Club*
  by Amy Tan

ITINERARY

FRIDAY
Lands End Trail
Tadich Grill martini lunch
City Lights Books

....

SATURDAY
Embarcadero jog
Japantown browse
SFJazz Center show
Frances dinner

....

SUNDAY
Tartine
Muir Woods hike
SFMOMA
Sam Wo dinner

MEMENTOS

Designing San Francisco by Alison Isenberg, $38
Reserve extra virgin olive oil, *Stonehouse*, $32
Plunge beach towel, *General Store*, $80

RECORD COLLECTION

Grateful Dead	*American Beauty*
Mac Dre	*The Game is Thick, Vol. 2*
Thao & The Get Down Stay Down	*Temple*
Dead Kennedys	*Fresh Fruit for Rotting Vegetables*
Jefferson Airplane	*Surrealistic Pillow*
E-40	*In a Major Way*
Santana	*Santana*
Sly and the Family Stone	*Stand!*
Big Brother and the Holding Company	*Cheap Thrills*
Third Eye Blind	*Third Eye Blind*
Steve Miller Band	*Fly Like an Eagle*
Chet Baker	*It Could Happen to You*
Huey Lewis and the News	*Sports*
Vince Guaraldi Trio	*Jazz Impressions of Black Orpheus*

ESSENTIALS

LODGING

Phoenix Hotel
601 Eddy St
Big-hearted, rock-themed mod motel in Tenderloin. Coffee's always on.
....

Inn at the Presidio
42 Moraga Ave
Salute yourself in elegant former officers quarters dating to 1903.
....

Hotel Drisco
2901 Pacific Ave
Cozy and crisply designed Pac Heights boutique.

Hotel Fairmont
950 Mason St
Old-school grandeur with an SF touch [onsite beehives].
....

White Swan Inn
845 Bush St
Wild design evokes England, filtered through a mind-blown '60s trip.
....

Hotel Kabuki
1625 Post St
Japantown winner. Sleek, big views, walk everywhere.

Cavallo Point
601 Murray Circle, Sausalito
Vintage luxe digs by the Bay. Quick to city and trail.
....

Manka's Inverness Lodge
10 Callendar Way, Inverness
Much loved woodsy cabins.
....

Ameswell
800 Moffett Blvd, Mountain View
Art-heavy Silicon Valley base.

WELLNESS

South End Rowing Club
A deeply historic sporting society, with club swims, intro rowing programs and famed handball courts. *500 Jefferson St*
....

Archimedes Banya
Russian hot massage, sauna and spa retreat. *748 Innes Ave*
....

Mission Cliffs
The city's venerable climbing gym, with scores of routes and classes for many levels. *2295 Harrison St*
....

Studio Velo
Over the Golden Gate, a source for top-notch cycling gear and clutch Headlands and Mount Tam routes. *31 Miller Ave, Mill Valley*

de Young Museum
Deep strength in the arts of the Americas, 1600s to contemporary works.

....

Museum of the African Diaspora
A global outlook on Black art. Excellent photo shows.

....

Mission Cultural Center for Latino Arts
Noted center for printmaking and performance.

....

Walt Disney Family Museum
The Mouseman's legacy, and beyond.

SFMOMA
A fizzy center of modern creativity in stunner building inspired by fog.

....

Berggruen Gallery
A blue-chip outfit. Heavy names, Currin to Frankenthaler to Ruscha and more.

....

Yerba Buena Center for the Arts
Bastion of cutting-edge thought and ambition in many disciplines.

....

Asian Art Museum
Collection of pan-Pacific heft: more than 18,000 works.

Legion of Honor
A classic, Euro-leaning palace of sculpture, painting, decorative arts.

....

California Historical Society
Troves of throwback imagery and scholarly treasures.

....

Fraenkel Gallery
One of the eminent photography galleries. A core sample of great image-makers, Muybridge to Weems.

....

Beat Museum
Documents and ephemera of the literary hepcats.

The Fillmore
Shrine of 1960s rock, still cooking

....

War Memorial Opera House
Home court for opera and ballet

....

Davies Symphony Hall
A modern temple of acoustics

....

Brick & Mortar Music Hall
Cross-genre indie and underground

SFJAZZ Center
Celebrating history and what's next

....

Rickshaw Stop
Touring indie, local bands, DJ sets

....

ODC Theater
Contemporary dance instigator

....

Great American Music Hall
Ornate showcase since 1907

ESSENTIALS

BOOKSTORES

City Lights Books
261 Columbus Ave
The epicenter of the Beat moment and national literary pilgrimage site. Also, easy to forget, just a very good bookstore.

....

The Booksmith
1727 Haight St
A rambling treasure in the Haight bustle, with a deep stock of SF titles up front and an allied bar, Alembic, next door.

....

Green Apple Books
506 Clement St
Nirvana for serious bookfolk, with new and used finds by the pile, a stacked events lineup and reliable staff picks.

....

Argonaut Book Shop
786 Sutter St
An archivist's delight, with antiquarian specialties in California and U.S. West history. The braintrust here dates back to 1941.

Book Passage
1 Ferry Building
Well known for its buzzing program of events and writing classes. Let Aunt Lydia pick out a title for you.

....

Omnivore Books on Food
3885 Cesar Chavez St
The culinary specialist, with a fine lineup of new cooking magazines, old cookbooks and vintage menus.

....

Alley Cat Bookstore & Gallery
3036 24th St
Serving the Mission in English and Spanish. Owner Kate Razo also runs beloved Dog Eared.

....

William Stout Architectural Books
804 Montgomery St
Get seriously brainy with an unmatched selection of monographs, magazines and books on design, homes and cities.

COFEEE

Sightglass
270 7th St

....

Linea Caffe
3417 18th St

....

Caffe Trieste
601 Vallejo St

....

Snowbird Coffee
1352 9th Ave A

....

Newkirk's
1002 Potrero Ave

....

Trouble Coffee
4033 Judah St

....

Excelsior Coffee
4495 Mission St

....

Flywheel
672 Stanyan St

....

Andytown Coffee Roasters
3655 Lawton St

....

The Mill
736 Divisadero St

....

Jane
925 Larkin St

....

Sextant
1415 Folsom St

ISSUES

Cost of Living	Skyrocketing housing prices driven by the tech boom help fuel SF's notorious expense. So do California's regulatory maze, NIMBY sentiment, and the city's small size, all making new housing hard to build. **EXPERT:** *Fernando Martí, co-director, Council of Community Housing Organizations*
Mental Health	Many people experiencing homelessness here also live with mental illness and substance abuse: recent city data shows about 4,000 San Franciscans facing all three. Advocates push for more treatment beds. **EXPERT:** *Steve Fields, director, Progress Foundation*
Air Quality	Climate change is worsening California wildfires. Flames haven't reached the city, but smoke has, creating hazardous air and an infamous September 2020 day of eerie orange skies. The city aims for net-zero carbon emissions by 2050. **EXPERT:** *Debbie Raphael, director, SF Environment*
Street Life	A rare coronavirus upside: the city of fog became an outdoor dining town. Parklets, patios and more walkable main streets livened the cityscape and, some say, softened SF's personality. Discussions about what's next evoke a long history of public festivals, parades and pocket parks. **EXPERT:** *Elizabeth Ranieri, design principal, Kuth Ranieri Architects*

STATISTICS

69	Career games, 49ers quarterback Colin Kaepernick
< 20%	Silicon Valley's 2021 share, national VC money [all-time low]
$1.8M	Median home price, spring 2021
33%	Recent decline in annual fog coverage, per 2010 study
25	Top speed [mph] of a California sea lion
6.9 : 7.9	Richter scale magnitude, 1989 quake vs. 1906 quake
16.4M	Total passengers at SFO, 2020
$1B	Google affordable housing funding pledge, 2019
2,300	Approximate career concerts, Grateful Dead

NEIGHBORHOODS

HAIGHT-ASHBURY

Summer of Love HQ. Victorians border Golden Gate Park, with counterculture on reboot.

LOCAL: *Distractions, Zam Zam*

....

PACIFIC HEIGHTS

Landmarks [Spreckels Mansion] dot a wealthy hilltop.

LOCAL: *Alta Plaza, b. patisserie*

....

OUTER SUNSET

Pacific fog rolls over low-slung beachfront streets.

LOCAL: *Old Mandarin Islamic, Pineapple King Bakery*

....

BERNAL HEIGHTS

Residential rise with a vigorous community tradition.

LOCAL: *Barebottle Brewing, Wild Side West, Piqueo's*

....

NOB HILL

Home to 1860s rail tycoons, forever desired real estate.

LOCAL: *Mikkeller Bar, Serafina, Union Square, Le Beau Market*

....

FINANCIAL DISTRICT

High-rise heart of SF hustle.

LOCAL: *Punch Line SF*

NORTH BEACH

Vintage Italian quarter, the Beat Generation's safe harbor.

LOCAL: *Vesuvio, Libreria Pino, Molinari Delicatessen*

....

JAPANTOWN

A six-block modernist enclave sprinkled with cherry blossoms.

LOCAL: *Books Kinokuniya*

....

MISSION

Murals and activist energy light up SF's Latino crossroads.

LOCAL: *Taqueria Cancun, Craftsmen and Wolves, The Sycamore*

....

CHINATOWN

Dragon's Gate marks North America's oldest Chinatown.

LOCAL: *Li Po Cocktail Lounge, Golden Gate Fortune Cookie*

....

RICHMOND

Gaze on the bridge [if fog lifts].

LOCAL: *Trad'r Sam, Mandalay*

....

CASTRO

Gilbert Baker first unfurled the rainbow flag here in 1978.

LOCAL: *Twin Peaks Tavern, Kitchen Story, Beaux, Hi Tops*

SAN FRANCISCO NEIGHBORHOODS ➡

MARINA

NORTH BEACH

RUSSIAN HILL

PRESIDIO

COW HOLLOW

CHINATOWN

PACIFIC HEIGHTS

NOB HILL

FINANCIAL
DISTRICT

LAUREL HEIGHTS   JAPANTOWN

TENDERLOIN

EMBARCADERO ≥

INNER RICHMOND

NOPA   HAYES VALLEY

SOMA

OUTER RICHMOND

HAIGHT ASHBURY

DUBOCE TRIANGLE

COLE VALLEY

POTRERO HILL

INNER SUNSET   CASTRO   MISSION

OUTER SUNSET

DOGPATCH ≥

TWIN PEAKS

NOE VALLEY

BERNAL HEIGHTS

PARKSIDE

BAYVIEW

LAKE MERCED   SUNNYSIDE

PORTOLA

MORE THAN 90 PICKS ☞

BESTS

A curated list of city favorites—classic and new—
from bars and restaurants to shops and experiences,
plus a handful of surefire experts.

FOOD & DRINK

NEIGHBORHOOD CAFE

Outerlands

4001 Judah Street
Outer Sunset

The driftwood café lays out crusty breads to cool every night. Granola and goat yogurt, avocado toast.

....

OYSTERS

Swan Oyster Depot

1517 Polk Street
Nob Hill

Fresh Dungeness, chowder and briny bivalves served to the same 18 seats at the counter since 1912, with 1890s roots.

....

HAWAIIAN

Liholiho Yacht Club

871 Sutter St
Nob Hill

Pan-Pacific vibes with the Okinawan Sour cocktail.

CALIFORNIAN

Frances

3870 17th St
Castro
frances-sf.com

Chef Melissa Perello's corner jewel serves bacon beignets and house table wine with its own cult.

....

VEGAN

Wildseed

2000 Union St
Cow Hollow

Curried cauliflower, Bolognese made with Impossible Burger, other meatless flavor blasts: an empire in the making.

....

BURRITO

La Taqueria

2889 Mission St
Mission

Among many burrito contenders, the riceless winner.

ITALIAN

Cotogna

490 Pacific Ave
Jackson Square

The Italic offshoot of chef Michael Tusk's lauded Cali spot, Quince. Lavish Florentine steak, but pizza, too.

....

DIM SUM

Good Luck Dim Sum

736 Clement St
Inner Richmond

Try the har gow, fun kor, turnip cake and sticky ball rice laced with pork. Line up and bring cash.

....

BAR & GRILL

Balboa Cafe

3199 Fillmore St
Marina

Gavin's spot. [You know Gavin.] Killer shrimp cocktail.

STEAKS

House of Prime Rib
1906 Van Ness Ave
Nob Hill
Stiff martinis and
thick cuts of beef,
carved tableside.

....

ROASTED CHICKEN

Zuni Café
1658 Market St
Hayes Valley
Yardbird roasted for
an hour, served with
dandelion greens.

....

VIETNAMESE

Claws of Mantis
@clawsofmantis
A closely tracked pop-
up, dropping intense
Viet/Cali menus via
Instagram.

....

BAKERY

Tartine Bakery
600 Guerrero St
Mission
Cultish breads, sweet
morning buns, fluffy
croissants.

....

ARAB COMFORT

Beit Rima
138 Church St
Castro
An ex-burger joint
reborn as a Palestin-
ian showcase, pulled
off with panache.

BREAKFAST SANDO

Devil's Teeth
3876 Noriega St
Outer Sunset
Buttermilk biscuit
wake-up call.

....

THE CLASSIC

Tadich Grill
240 California St
Financial District
Dimly lit portal to
SF of yore. Always
the same waiters.
Always the crab.

CHICKEN AND WAFFLES

Little Skillet
360 Ritch St
China Basin
Southern warmth
amid the fog: two
pieces, a waffle and
side for under $20.

....

TASTING MENU

Coi
373 Broadway
Jackson Square
Daniel Patterson's
big-money bites of
ocean and farm.

....

MEXICAN

Loló
974 Valencia St
Mission
Jalisco menu meets
California ingredi-
ents and style.

WINE LIST

Nopa
560 Divisadero St
Alamo Square
Restaurant folk
flock to the 200-plus
list of wise Euro and
Cali picks.

....

DIVE BAR

New Judnich's
2888 San Bruno Ave
Portola
Zero scene, and
that's the point.

....

WINE BAR

Union Larder
1945 Hyde St
Russian Hill
Colossal by-the-glass
list, many on tap,
mostly Californian.

....

TIKI

Last Rites
718 14th St
Duboce Triangle
Dreamy drinks, de-
cor, from respected
Horsefeather crew.

....

COCKTAILS

Propagation
895 Post St
Lower Nob Hill
Creative drinks in
a sun-kissed, leafy
room. Hammett
wrote *Falcon* upstairs.

SHOPPING

TABLETOP
Heath Ceramics
2900 18th St
Mission
Firing kilns since 1948, inspiring kitchen dreams with a distinctly California aesthetic.
....

HOME
March
3075 Sacramento St
Pacific Heights
Sophisticated kitchenware and furniture, both modern and classic.
....

WINESHOP
Ruby Wine
1419 18th St
Potrero Hill
Neighborhood-scale coziness but a citywide rep for natural wines picked by a staff of enthusiasts.

JAPANESE HARDWARE
Soko Hardware
1698 Post St
Japantown
An intergenerational shop stocked with Japanese tools, a combination of the beautiful and handy.
....

CLOGS
Bryr
2331 3rd St
Dogpatch
Maker studio invested in vintage Cali style, green materials and, well, great clogs.
....

OLD PRINT
The Magazine SF
920 Larkin St
Tenderloin
Rare magazines of classic *Life* vintage and rich ephemera. On guard: there's some naughty stuff.

LIFESTYLE
General Store
4035 Judah St
Outer Sunset
Sunny sundries curated with Joan Didion's sensibility and Alice Waters' taste level.
....

VINYL
Amoeba Records
1855 Haight St
Haight-Ashbury
Collector's godsend. Staff picks lead down many a delightful rabbit hole.
....

DISCOVERIES
The Perish Trust
728 Divisadero St
NoPa
theperishtrust.com
Industrial antiques and new finds. Founded by artists, and it shows.

MENSWEAR

Taylor Stitch
383 Valencia St
Mission
Launched with the aim to perfect the button-down shirt.

....

HORNS

Lee's Sax Worx
1724 Taraval St
Sunset
Vintage brass and repairs, plus the most amazing website.

....

CO-OP

Rainbow Grocery
1745 Folsom St
Mission
Employee-owned since 1975. The cheese case is a true worker's paradise.

....

JEWELRY

Reliquary
544 Hayes St
Hayes Valley
One-of-a-kind pieces, small design lines.

....

AQUARIUMS

Aqua Forest
1718 Fillmore St
Japantown
SF's aquascaping experts, notable for bringing minimalist style to tank design.

DESIGN SUPPLY

Arch
1490 17th St
Potrero Hill
Hub for working artists—board cutting, pen cleaning, replacement parts.

....

POTIONS

The Sword and Rose
85 Carl St
Cole Valley
Ivy-covered sanctum of botanical wisdom.

....

PAPER GOODS

Rare Device
600 Divisadero St
NoPa
Whimsical gifting and stationary.

....

PROVISIONS

Little Vine
1541 Grant Ave
Telegraph Hill
Artisanal cheeses, charcuterie, floor-to-ceiling wine selection.

....

WONDERS

Paxton Gate
824 Valencia St
Mission
An explorer's trove of framed butterflies, taxidermy exotica. Gifts for eccentrics.

WOMENSWEAR

Uko
350 Hayes St
Western Addition
Launched to showcase Japanese styles, now sourcing global snappy-casual looks.

....

VINTAGE

Relic
1605 Haight St
Haight-Ashbury
Midcentury fashions with verve.

....

USED INSTRUMENTS

Real Guitars
15 Lafayette St
SoMa
Vintage and custom-built axes.

....

GEAR

Mission Workshop
40 Rondel Pl
Mission
Bomb-proof backpacks and apparel rated for your next trip into the field.

....

MAKERS

Woodshop
3725 Noriega St
Outer Sunset
Handcrafted wooden surfboards, furniture and more, from four distinct designers.

ACTION

HIKING
Mt Tamalpais
Mill Valley
parksconservancy.org
Redwood valleys, creeks, waterfalls, 360 views and miles of secluded trails.
....

INDIE FILMMAKING
Ninth Street Independent Film Center
SoMa
ninthstreet.org
Huge base for DIY creation, with a public screening room and many editing stations.
....

SECRET BEACH
Pirates Cove
West Marin
From Muir Beach, hike Coastal Fire Road 1.5 miles to a white-sand former bootlegger's hideout.

BOTANICAL WANDER
Flora Grubb Gardens
1634 Jerrold Ave
floragrubb.com
As much a vibe as a plant shop. Commune with greenery.
....

LITERARY CULTURE
Quiet Lightning
quietlightning.org
A vibrant nexus of new Bay Area voices. Live events both IRL and online, plus original publications, art and writer interviews.
....

KIDS
Helen Diller Playground
Mission Dolores Park
State-of-the-art acre of romping, climbing fun. Home of the Super Slide.

CYCLING
Rapha Clubhouse
2198 Filbert St
Cow Hollow
The racy road gear brand's SF base is a handy take-off for Marin rides.
....

SWIMMING HOLE
The Inkwells
West Marin
8889 Sir Francis
Drake Blvd
Boulder-strewn pools, cold and deep, along Lagunitas Creek, just inside Taylor State Park.
....

ARCADE
Musée Mécanique
Fisherman's Wharf
museemecanique.org
Slot machines of yore. Meet "Laughing Sal" and the gypsy fortuneteller.

BREWERY TOUR
Anchor
1705 Mariposa St
Potrero Hill
anchorbrewing.com
Craft brewing's oldest
of the old school.

....

CITY PARK
Mount Davidson
Sherwood Forest
bahiker.com
SF's highest point,
best when fog veils
the eucalyptus.

....

ROLLER RINK
Church of 8 Wheels
554 Fillmore St
Lower Haight
Roll in a former
church run by com-
mitted [fanatical?]
skater David Miles.

....

LIVE EVENT
Pop-Up Magazine
popupmagazine.com
Founded here, this
live-journalism show
went national.

....

SURF SPOT
Ocean Beach
Outer Sunset
aquasurfshop.com
Clean lines and
cold water, triple
overhead on biggest
days. Seriously.

NIGHTLIFE
Madrone Art Bar
500 Divisadero St
NoPa
madroneartbar.com
Artists new and old
and soulful DJ sets.

....

DRAG SHOW
Aunt Charlie's
133 Turk St
Tenderloin
The Hot Boxxx Girls
go live at 10, Friday
and Saturday.

....

GETAWAY
Tomales Bay
23240 CA Hwy 1
nickscove.com
Oyster shacks, Point
Reyes exploring and
serene cottages at
Nick's Cove.

....

FESTIVAL
Hardly Strictly
Bluegrass
Golden Gate Park
Banjos come out
every October. Free.

....

DOG DAY
Fort Funston
Lakeshore
nps.gov
Sand bluffs rising
200 feet, tree groves,
open beach, off-leash
romping.

SPORTS BAR
Final Final
1990 Baker St
Cow Hollow
Family-run sporting
palace decked with
screens and curios.

....

PLAYHOUSE
ACT
act-sf.org
Shows at the historic
Geary Theater, plus
acclaimed acting
classes for all.

....

OUTDOOR SHOWS
Stern Grove
Sunset District
sterngrove.org
Decades of free con-
certs. Vince Guaraldi
in '66, Perfume
Genius in '21.

....

TENNIS
Alice Marble Courts
Greenwich and Hyde
Russian Hill
Four courts way up
the hill. Stunning
city and bay views.

....

KARAOKE
Festa
1825 A Post St
Japantown
Cozy nook with deep
catalogues of Eng-
lish and global hits.

EXPERTISE

GROCER
Bi-Rite Market
biritemarket.com
The miniature grocery chain that has its own farm, nonprofit program and grants for organizations doing good.
....

CHOCOLATES
Dandelion
dandelionchocolate.com
A small factory roasting beans from single-source partners around the world to create enviable artisan bars.
....

DENIM REPAIR
Self Edge
selfedge.com
Blue jean obsessives started here in the City of Levi's. Fixing scuffs, rips, blowouts for a $40 flat rate.

FASHION
Chinatown Pretty
@chinatownpretty
Andria Lo and Valerie Luu wrote the book on vibrant fashions sported by Chinatown seniors. A glorious follow.
....

HIV/AIDS
Paul Volberding
ucsf.edu
Early '80s post at SF General put him at the epidemic's heart. Since then, decades of research and editing of key journals.
....

BIKE REPAIR
Andrés Hernández Rojo
speedycorona.com
Painter and photographer fixes just about any ride out of a Balmy Alley garage.

FOOD START-UPS
La Cocina
lacocinasf.org
Access to kitchen space and business know-how boosts minority-owned restaurant launches. National inspiration.
....

CITY PLANNING
SPUR
spur.org
Ambitious urban ideas inside a gleaming HQ. Check out the deep-dive project to envision the Bay Area in 2070.
....

STYLING
Kendra Smoot
kendrasmoot.com
Sparkling-fresh photo styling and art direction. Clients include *Bon App*, *Cookie* and *Kinfolk*.

FOOD CRITIC

Soleil Ho

soleilho.com

Since 2019, charting culinary, cultural and political crosscurrents for the *Chronicle*.

....

FILMMAKER

Joe Talbot

longshotfeatures.com

Founder of Longshot studio, director of *The Last Black Man in San Francisco*, tracker of SF essence.

....

PODCAST

Fifth & Mission

sfchronicle.com

The *Chron*'s flagship politics pod romps through the weeds of Bay Area and statewide issues.

....

SPACE DESIGN

Rapt Studio

raptstudio.com

Stellar workspaces for brands like The North Face, Google and Goop.

....

DIGITAL HISTORY

Internet Archive

archive.org

Wayback Machine resides in a grand HQ on Funston.

MARINE ECOLOGY

William Sydeman

faralloninstitute.org

Institute founder began as a seabird specialist on Farallon Islands in 1981.

....

SOMMELIER

Tonya Pitts

@noirsommelier

A writer and speaker as well as a seasoned palette, she's a national force in wine.

....

WATCH REPAIR

Independent Watch Service Center

415-982-9830

When your Oyster's on the fritz, the esteemed Passalacqua family can help.

....

TATTOO

Idle Hand

idlehandsf.com

Haight's go-to ink stop, steeped in San Francisco's rich tattooing history.

....

SOCIAL ADVOCACY

Glide Church

glide.org

Beloved liberal beacon championing the disenfranchised.

KNIFE SHARPENING

Bernal Cutlery

bernalcutlery.com

Japanese sharpening techniques tailored to the blade's intended use.

....

LANDSCAPE ARCHITECT

Janet Hankinson

janethankinson.com

Thirty-plus years of lush Bay Area grounds, notable for blending native and edible plants.

....

MAP DESIGN

Stamen

stamen.com

Data artists visualize global issues for clients like Google, Toyota. Maps available for online use.

....

MECHANIC

Toy Shop

415-386-0122

Trustworthy to the point of being perpetually slammed. Ask for Wayland.

....

FOG

Karl the Fog

@karlthefog

Documenting murks and mists, maybe even sun.

MORE THAN 30 ENTRIES ▷
Excerpts have been edited for clarity and concision.

ALMANAC

A deep-dive into the cultural heritage of San Francisco, featuring Mark Twain's and Jack London's journalism, the Wiggle, the Summer of Love, Japanese internment, jazz clubs, Beat poets and more.

THE 1906 EARTHQUAKE

"The Story of an Eyewitness"
by Jack London

After being telegrammed by Collier's *magazine, London and his wife Charmian traveled by horse into the burning city to document the disaster. The excerpts below are part of his 2,500-word reportage.*

Not in history has a modern imperial city been so completely destroyed. San Francisco is gone. Nothing remains of it but memories and a fringe of dwelling-houses on its outskirts.

....

The smoke of San Francisco's burning was a lurid tower visible a hundred miles away. And for three days and nights this lurid tower swayed in the sky, reddening the sun, darkening the day, and filling the land with smoke.

....

Streets were humped into ridges and depressions, and piled with the debris of fallen walls. All the shrewd contrivances and safeguards of man had been thrown out of gear by thirty seconds' twitching of the earth-crust.

....

Wednesday night, while the whole city crashed and roared into ruin, was a quiet night. I passed Wednesday night in the path of the advancing flames, and in all those terrible hours I saw not one woman who wept. They held on longest to their trunks, and over these trunks many a strong man broke his heart that night. The hills of San Francisco are steep, and up these hills, mile after mile, were the trunks dragged.

....

Here the shopkeepers and soft members of the middle class were at a disadvantage. But the working-men dug holes in vacant lots and backyards and buried their trunks.

....

"Yesterday morning," he said, "I was worth six hundred thousand dollars. This morning this house is all I have left. It will go in fifteen minutes.... Try that piano. Listen to its tone. There are few like it."

....

San Francisco, at the present time, is like the crater of a volcano, around which are camped tens of thousands of refugees.

DIMAGGIO

The Los Angeles Times
May 1, 1934

Chief interest in the Seals will be centered on the arrival here of "The Great" Mails, who admits being an attraction in himself, and "Dead Pan" DiMaggio, the sensational young slugger. Mails does all the talking for the club while DiMaggio does most of the hitting. They say DiMaggio is bigger and better this year. He grew more than an inch and added fifteen pounds to his frame during the winter and the Seals are getting ready to place a $100,000 price tag on him. In case you have forgotten, Joe is the lad who hit safely in sixty-one consecutive games for a world's record last season. But hitting isn't his only virtue. DiMaggio also fields superbly and throws with the best of them.

> *Giuseppe Paolo DiMaggio—Joltin' Joe, the Yankee Clipper—grew up in San Francisco, the son of a fisherman. Joe and his brothers Vince and Dom worked on the boats as boys, hauling nets and strengthening what would become a trio of Major League outfield arms. Joe had a 13-year career with the Yankees, joining the team from the San Francisco Seals club in 1936, and he went on to win nine World Series championships and four batting titles. Ted Williams called DiMaggio the greatest right-handed hitter of all time. After retiring, Joe split time between Florida and his hometown, until his death in 1999.*

THE SISTERS OF PERPETUAL INDULGENCE (PAST AND PRESENT)

Protest performance troupe started in 1979 to combat sexual intolerance.

· Sister Hysterectoria
· Sister Secuba
· Sister Barbi Mitzvah
· Sister Eve Volution
· Sister Hellen Wheels of the Daughters of Divine Eruption
· Sister OyVey Maria
· Sister Florence Nightmare
· Sister Roma! There's No Place Like Rome
· Sister Risqué of the Sissytine Chapel

GOLD RUSH

CALIFORNIAN
By B.R. Buckelew
San Francisco, March 15, 1848

GOLD MINE FOUND.- In the newly made raceway of the Saw Mill recently erected by Captain Sutter, on the American Fork, gold has been found in considerable quantities. One person brought thirty dollars worth to New Helvetia, gathered there in a short time. California, no doubt, is rich in mineral wealth; great chances here for scientific capitalists. Gold has been found in almost every part of the country.

JOE MONTANA

Hall of Fame 49ers QB

year	yds	td	record
1979	96	1	0-1
1980	1795	15	2-5
1981	3565	19	13-3*
1982	2613	17	3-6
1983	3910	26	10-6
1984	3630	28	14-1*
1985	3653	27	9-6
1986	2236	8	6-2
1987	3054	31	10-1
1988	2981	18	8-5*
1989	3521	26	11-2*
1990	3944	26	14-1
1991	0	0	0-0
1992	126	2	0-0**

*Super Bowl Champions
**An elbow injury kept him sidelined for all of 1991 and all but one half of 1992

COPPOLA

In 1969, ten years before Apocalypse Now debuted, director Francis Ford Coppola approached Oscar-winner Lee Marvin for the role that would later be made famous by Marlon Brando.

American Zoetrope
827 Folsom Street
San Francisco, CA 94107

Mr. Lee Marvin,
We'd like you to play the part of Colonel Karnage in Apocalypse Now. We're an independant company in San Francisco financed by Warner Bros. It's a good script.

Sincerely,
Francis Ford Coppola

RISE OF TECHNOLOGY

1909	Federal Telegraph Co. created in Palo Alto
1927	All-electronic television broadcasting invented in SF
1939	Walt Disney is Hewlett-Packard's first customer
1955	Shockley Transistor Lab founded in Mountain View
1956	IBM builds hard-disk drive in San Jose
1959	Sherman Fairchild starts semiconductor company
1961	Robert Noyce invents microchip
1961	IBM is 81% of computer market
1963	Prototype of the first "mouse"
1968	Memory chip company Intel founded
1972	Video game *Pong* released by Atari
1976	Dolby Labs moves to SF from Great Britain
1976	Steve Jobs and Steve Wozniak begin Apple in garage
1977	Larry Ellison starts Oracle
1980	Apple IPO, $1.3 billion
1983	Paul Mockapetris invents domain name system
1984	Apple releases its revolutionary Macintosh
1985	Jobs leaves Apple, buys Pixar a year later
1988	Internet infested with "Morris," first digital worm
1994	Jerry and David's Guide to the World Wide Web, a.k.a. Yahoo!
1995	Netscape goes public, starts the dot-com boom
1995	Craig Newmark starts smalltime advertising co-op
1995	Broken laser pointer, first item sold on eBay
1996	Steve Jobs back to Apple, Jony Ive as design lead
1997	Netflix dooms the movie rental industry
1998	America Online acquires Netscape
1998	Stanford students, Brin and Page, start Google
1999	Napster launches
2000	Pets.com shuts down, signals end of dot-com boom
2001	The first iPod, "1,000 songs in your pocket"
2003	Virtual "Second Life"
2004	Facebook moves from Harvard to Palo Alto
2006	Google buys YouTube
2009	Ashton Kutcher, Twitter's first to a million followers
2010	iPad debuts, Facebook hits 500 million users
2011	Steve Jobs dies, described as modern Edison
2016	Russian hackers breach DNC election campaign systems
2021	Jan. 6 insurrection, Trump banned from Twitter, Facebook

COMMITTEE OF VIGILANCE

In 1851, lawlessness afflicted a booming San Francisco, much attributed to Australian criminals known as "Sydney Ducks." Several hundred people vowed to take matters in hand.

CONSTITUTION.
9th June 1851.

Whereas it has become apparent to the Citizens of San Francisco that there is no security for life and property either under the regulations of Society as it at present exists or under the laws as now administered,— therefore, the Citizens whose names are hereunto attached do unite themselves into an association for the maintenance of the peace and good order of Society and the preservation of the lives and property of the Citizens of San Francisco and do bind ourselves each unto the other to do and perform every lawful act for the maintenance of law and order and to sustain the laws when faithfully and properly administered but we are determined that no thief burglar incendiary or assassin shall escape punishment, either by the quibbles of the law the insecurity of prisons the carelessness or corruption of the Police or a laxity of those who pretend to administer justice.

The original San Francisco vigilantes executed Australians John Jenkins [accused burglar] and James Stuart [murder] and killed or exiled others. Violence flared again in 1856, deeply influencing the city politics of the time.

FOG

A simple explanation of the city's summer weather.

1. From April into June, Pacific High anticyclone moves north
2. Cold water rises, causing condensation
3. Central Valley summer temps hit 100 degrees
4. Hot air in low-lying towns rises
5. Cool sea air sucked inland
6. Coastal mountains block fog, SF Bay is natural break
7. At max, million tons of water an hour move through as fog
8. Valley cools into the 90s, fog disappears
9. Three or four days of sun, fog machine starts up again

INTERNATIONAL ORANGE

*When city officials debated on a color for the Golden Gate Bridge,
the case was made that the steel primer already on the towers would
be the best complement to the green hills, blue skies and the summer fog
blankets. Today the one-of-a-kind paint lives in an underground bunker,
enough to cover more than 10 million square feet of surface area,
and a 28-man team of painters retouch the bridge continuously,
though the Sisyphean myth of endless end-to-end work is not quite reality.
What's true—architect Irving Morrow made the right color call.
Below, an excerpt from his 29-page case for international orange.*

**THE GOLDEN GATE BRIDGE:
REPORT ON COLOR AND
LIGHTING (APRIL 6, 1935)**

1. Local Atmospheric Effects

During summer, the San Francisco Bay area is covered by high fogs and is relatively sunless. At these times the atmosphere is gray. In sunny weather the predominant color of bay and ocean is blue. In other words, the prevalent atmospheric colors are cool. A structure which is to be emphasized must appear in contrasting or warm colors.

2. The Color

Except during the transitory Panama-Pacific International Exposition of 1915, local architecture has remained on the whole timidly colorless, hence without the accent and warmth which conditions call for.

The colors which meet the above requirements range through yellow, orange and red. Not all, however, are equally appropriate from other points of view. Yellow shades would lack substance: deep reds would be heavy and without luminosity.

During the erection of the north tower, and again at the present moment with the south tower assuming form, observers from all walks of life have been universally impressed by the beauty of the structures in the shop red lead coat. This color is luminous, undergoes atmospheric changes with great beauty, is prominent without insistence, enhances the architectural scale to the utmost and gives weight and substance at the same time. ... In short, it is the ideal color from every point of view, and is hereby recommended and urged as the most appropriate and satisfactory color for the finished bridge.

THE DIGGERS PAPERS

Fall 1966

LET ME LIVE IN A WORLD PURE
LET ME HAVE AROUND ME
THE PURE
THE PURE HEROES

there are no more negroes, jews, christians. there is only one minority in America. and we ask:

When will BOB DYLAN quit working on Maggie's Farm?

When will RALPH GLEASON realize he is riding in a Hearst?

When will TIMOTHY LEARY stand on a streetcorner waiting for no one?

When will the JEFFERSON AIRPLANE and all ROCK-GROUPS quit trying to make it and LOVE?

When will NORMAN MAILER fill his brooklyn town house with presses and feed words to a day-tight night-tight generation?

When will OSWLEY [sic] STANLEY expose the traffic of alkaline acid and pour his background into LSD-25?

When will the NEW LEFT RADICAL POLITICS stop laying down limp and liberate the consumer?

When will PABLO PICASSO take the seven thousand paintings he has in storage and give them away with a smile?

When will KEN KESEY swallow the ocean and take us all to Yucatan?

When will MICHAEL BOWEN and friends use, look through, but not package the expansion of human consciousness?

When will ALLEN GINZBURG [sic] be blessed by his own seed and golden hairy nakedness?

When will ART-FOR-ART'S-SAKE climb higher than the social responsibility of the civilized past?

When will they all hear the death of LENNY BRUCE?

THE WIGGLE

To cycle from one side of the city to the other, locals follow the mile-long Wiggle bike path along the course of the old Sans Souci Creek, a waterway that flowed through the area when the city was still known as Yerba Buena. The Wiggle's uncharacteristic flatness has garnered it traffic for hundreds of years, from the Indigenous Ohlone to the Spanish explorers to the current armies of helmet-clad and backpack-wielding commuters. To wiggle, follow the zigzagging green arrows from the end of the Panhandle to Duboce Park or vice versa—regardless of direction, you'll encounter a welcome reprieve from the city's more unforgiving gradients.

HOW TO WIGGLE:

1. Start at Duboce and Market
2. Right on Steiner
3. Left on Waller
4. Right on Pierce
5. Left on Haight
6. Right on Scott
7. Left on Fell

FILLMORE JAZZ CLUBS

Between the years of 1940 and 1950, the Black population in San Francisco grew from 4,846 people to over 43,000. Thousands migrated to work in the city's shipyards, which boomed during World War II. The Fillmore District became the epicenter of Black cultural life, and became known as the "Harlem of the West." Jazz clubs opened throughout the area, and saw the likes of Charlie Parker, Billie Holiday, Dizzy Gillespie and Dexter Gordon. Almost none of these clubs survived past the 1960s, when the city government issued a redevelopment plan that effectively decimated large swaths of the neighborhood.

- ≥ New Orleans Swing Club
- ≥ Texas Playhouse
- ≥ Jimbo's Bop City
- ≥ The Champagne Supper Club
- ≥ Leola King's Blue Mirror
- ≥ Jack's Tavern
- ≥ Club Alabam
- ≥ Both/And
- ≥ The Long Bar
- ≥ Vout City
- ≥ Minnie's Can-Do Club
- ≥ Elsie's Breakfast Nook
- ≥ Blackshear's Cafe Society
- ≥ The Favorite

HARVEY MILK

*Excerpted below are two speeches made by Harvey Milk.
The first is a campaign speech in which Milk announced his
candidacy for the District 5 seat of the San Francisco Board
of Supervisors. The second is a speech made at a fundraising
dinner, the day after Milk was inaugurated.*

"YOU'VE GOT TO HAVE HOPE"
JUNE 24, 1977

Let's go back to the beginning. I am announcing my candidacy for Supervisor of a great City. Think about that for a moment. A city isn't a collection of buildings—it isn't downtown with the B of A and a TransAmerica Tower, it isn't the parking lots or the freeways or the theaters or the massage parlors. A city is people. In this case some 675,000. Some 60,000 of them live in District 5. They're Latins and Blacks, whites and Chinese, young and old, straight—and gay. Each of these people has his or her own hopes and aspirations, his or her own viewpoints and problems. Each of them contributes something unique to the life of the city. What they contribute, we call the "quality of life."

"A CITY OF NEIGHBORHOODS"
JANUARY 10, 1978

I understand very well that my election was not alone a question of my gayness but a question of what I represented. In a very real sense, Harvey Milk represented the spirit of the neighborhoods of San Francisco. ... Let's make no mistake about this: The American Dream starts with neighborhoods. If we wish to rebuild our cities, we must first rebuild our neighborhoods. And to that, we must understand that the quality of life is more important than the standard of living. To sit on the front steps—whether it's a veranda in a small town or a concrete stoop in a big city—and talk to our neighbors is infinitely more important than to huddle on the living room lounger and watch a make-believe world in not-quite living color.

NANCY PELOSI

Remarks Upon Becoming
Speaker of the House
Jan. 4, 2007

Thank you, my colleagues. Thank you, Leader Boehner, Mr. Speaker. I accept this gavel in the spirit of partnership, not partisanship, and I look forward to working ... [APPLAUSE] I look forward to working with you, Mr. Boehner, and the Republicans in the Congress, for the good of the American people. After giving this gavel away in the last two Congresses, I'm glad someone else has the honor today. [LAUGHTER] In this House, we may be different parties, but we serve one country. And our pride and our prayers are united behind our men and women in uniform. [APPLAUSE] They are working together to protect the American people. And in this Congress, we must work together to build a future worthy of their sacrifice. ... Forty-three years ago, Paul Pelosi and I were married. We raised our five children in San Francisco, where Paul was born and raised. I want to thank Paul and our five children—Nancy Corinne, Christine, Jacqueline, Paul Jr., and Alexandra—and our magnificent grandchildren—for their love, for their support, and the confidence they gave me to go from the kitchen to the Congress. [APPLAUSE] And I thank my constituents in San Francisco, and for the state of California, for the privilege of representing them in Congress. Saint Francis of Assisi is our city's patron saint. And his "Song of Saint Francis" is our city's anthem: "Lord, make me a channel of thy peace; where there is darkness may we bring light, where there is hatred, may we bring love, where is despair, may we bring hope." Hope: that is what America is about. And it is in that spirit that I serve in the Congress of the United States. [APPLAUSE] And today, I thank my colleagues. By electing me speaker, you have brought us closer to the ideal of equality that is America's heritage and America's hope. This is an historic moment. And I thank the leader for acknowledging it. Thank you, Mr. Boehner. It's an historic moment for the Congress. It's an historic moment for the women of America. [APPLAUSE] It is a moment for which we have waited over 200 years. [APPLAUSE]

THE SUMMER OF LOVE

A short, complicated history.

JAPANESE INTERNMENT

News coverage, Spring 1942

"JAPANESE WOMAN ATTEMPTS SUICIDE"
MARCH 18, 1942

Mrs. Edako Ono, Japanese, 41, 1354 Grant avenue, attempted suicide last night by walking into the ocean at the foot of Lincoln way. Passersby noticed the woman and called the Coast guardsmen who rescued her. At Park Emergency Hospital the woman's husband told attaches she was despondent because they are to be evacuated.

....

"JAP SCHOOLBOY CONFESSES TO A STABBING"
MARCH 27, 1942

Shinji Ono, 14-year-old Japanese Lowell High School student, yesterday confessed he stabbed Morris Gibbs, 67, hardware dealer at 2116 Fillmore street, "because he called me a Jap." Inspectors Joseph Lippi and Louis De Matei traced the youth by checking school records for absences. Gibbs identified the youth at a lineup of Japanese students at Lowell High School. Ono, who lives at 2105 Pierce street, readily confessed the assault.

....

"GOODBYE! WRITE SOON!" ALIEN EXODUS LIKE AN OUTING
APRIL 7, 1942

With a few courteous bows, lots of promises to "write soon" and many sturdy American-type handshakes, the first Japanese involved in military evacuation orders, yesterday said farewell to San Francisco. The elders, steeped in their native traditions, displayed few emotions. School-aged youngsters romped and played among the piles of household goods strewn in front of the control stations of the Wartime Civil Control Administration, 2020 and 1701 Van Ness-av. By taxi, streetcar, truck, van and in the autos of Occidental friends, the Japanese arrived with their suitcases, trunks and bundles of household goods. Late in the afternoon they boarded 10 buses, which took them to a special train.

LETTER FROM GINSBERG TO KEROUAC & CASSADY

San Francisco, CA
February 1952

Mon cher Jack, Mon Cher Neal!

Things is going great. Since I last wrote you I have been working steadily at typewriter piecing together mad poems—I have already 100 of them, I'm jumping. Listen to this: I'm putting together fragments of "Shroudy Stranger," with a small descriptive poem—to busy on fragments to get to the EPIC which will be next.

Now, what I want to know from you: my fantasies and phrases have gotten so lovingly mixed up in yours, Jack, I hardly know whose is which and who's used what: like rainfall's hood and moon is half yours. I am enclosing copies of poems that seem to stem from you, like rhetoric at the end of "Long Poem"—is "very summa and dove" yours? I'm not haggling I just want to know if it's OK to use anything I want that creeps in?

Spoke to [William Carlos] Williams on phone, go down to River Street tomorrow. He said he already (he hasn't seen the whole hundred, just about five poems) spoken with Random House (I thought it was going to be New Directions) and book may be there. Isn't this crazy? I've been off my nut with work and giggling.

....

SIX GALLERY READING

Friday, October 7, 1955, five young poets read their work in a salon-style setting on Fillmore Street. Jack Kerouac cheered from the crowd, which included Neal Cassady and City Lights' Lawrence Ferlinghetti. Below, the poets and their poems.

Allen Ginsberg .... "Howl"
Michael McClure .... "Point Lobos: Animism"
Gary Snyder .... "A Berry Feast"
Philip Whalen .... "Plus Ça Change"
Phillip Lamantia .... Poems by the late John Hoffman

PROSPECTOR'S JOURNAL

Charles T. Palmer

SUNDAY, SEPT. 22, 1850

Yesterday was a horrible day. It rained—poured rather—and completely drenched us all. The clouds seemed permanent and we determined to build us a roof. We worked all day in the rain. The moonlight was employed till one o'clock in discussing a bottle of brandy at the housewarming of our palace, which like that of Aladdin, had risen during the night.

....

SUNDAY, OCT. 27, 1850

Prospects begin now to look like a winter residence here. We have thought seriously about taking ourselves to San Francisco, but the cholera is there now, and this with other things may keep us here. In either case, we will be jolly.

....

THURSDAY, DEC. 5, 1850

A walk yesterday took me back of the Sugar Loaf, where we worked first. Our old claims were rooted up. Some new and quite rich ravines had been discovered, but generally the success was quite moderate. A small city with five stories has grown up in two months.

....

MONDAY, DEC 23, 1850

We are all well now and get the most possible out of Wood's Creek and Lawson's Ravine. We have times of queer jollity every night after work is over. At about midnight we turn in and listen to the conjugal debates between Ned and Charlie, such as who scratches Charlie's leg, and why Ned always will "spoon" up so close. Then till morning a solitary trombone peals forth a nasal blast.

....

SUNDAY, JAN. 26, 1851

Forward, March! We are going to San Francisco in hope that something will turn up. In other words —Roger is sick of the mines and I am ready for anything. I am not leaving the mines forever, a disappointed man. True—they have ruined me, but then they have dozen times come within an ace of making me, and they shall do it yet, unless I die untimely.

FOG SIGNALS

If New York has its taxi-and-siren song, San Francisco's background music has always been the fog signals scattered around the bay. When officials tried to replace the old standbys, the city became ill, longing for the familiar moans. As columnist Carl Nolte wrote of the Golden Gate horn in 1992, "It runs on compressed air and goes off on a precise schedule of its own, and sounds like the snort of some monster from the cold depths of the deepest ocean, a basso profundo from another world. Unwary motorists driving over the horn at the instant it sounds are occasionally lifted straight up from the car seat."

GOLDEN GATE BRIDGE, SOUTH PIER
Horn with two-second blast every 20 seconds

GOLDEN GATE BRIDGE, MID-SPAN
Three two-tone horns begin with nine-second pause, one-second blast, two-second pause, one-second blast, 36-second silence, one-second blast, two-second pause, one-second blast, 36-second silence; higher tones blast to the east, lower blasts to the west

GOLDEN GATE BRIDGE, LIME POINT
SuperTyfon horn sounds a two-second blast, silence for two seconds, another two-second blast, then 24 seconds of silence

MILE ROCKS
Air signal with one blast every 30 seconds

POINT DIABLO
Horn with one blast every 15 seconds

POINT BONITA
Identical to Lime Point, but facing seaward

ALCATRAZ, NORTH END
Two two-second blasts every 30 seconds

ALCATRAZ, SOUTH END
One three-second blast every 30 seconds

ANGEL ISLAND, POINT BLUNT
One two-second blast every 15 seconds

BAY BRIDGE
There are 11 fog signals on the piers, all a different combination of bells, horns and sirens

"I WILL SURVIVE!"

Nurse's Own 'Gay Cancer' Story

The Sentinel
December 10, 1981

I'm Bobbi Campbell, and I have "gay cancer." Although I say that, I also want to say that I'm the luckiest man in the world. Let me hasten to add that I'm not lucky *because* I have Kaposi's Sarcoma. I'm lucky and happy because in my time of crisis, I've found out who my real friends are. I'm surrounded by people who love me, who care about me, who follow my progress with interest, and who want me to get well soon.

Let me tell you something about myself. I'm a 29-year-old, white, gay man who's lived in the City for six years. I work as a Registered Nurse at Ralph K. Davies Medical Center, and I'm studying at the University of California at San Francisco [UCSF] for a Master's Degree in Nursing as an Adult Health Nurse Practitioner.

In September, my lover Ron and I went on a honeymoon car trip down the coast to Monterey, Big Sur, San Simeon, and the Pinnacles National Monument. When we returned, I took off my hiking boots, and surprise! On the soles of both feet I noticed purple, painless spots, about an inch in diameter. Since Ron and I had been hiking through some rough territory, I assumed that they were blood blisters and didn't pay any more attention to them.

Three weeks later, the lesions were still there. ["Lesion" is a broad medical term referring to any tissue breakdown or loss of function.] About that time, I was reading in the straight media about "gay cancer"—rare diseases that were mainly afflicting homosexual males. When my lover, who is a chiropractor, told me that Kaposi's Sarcoma usually occurred on the feet, I started to worry.

I've become so active in publicizing KS and the other gay illnesses to friends and media that I've taken to referring to myself sardonically as the "Kaposi's Sarcoma Poster Boy." True, I haven't received any offers from movie stars for telethon fundraisers, but I'm still available. My friend Gary thought that calling myself a "poster boy" showed a macabre sense of humor. Yes, Gary, I can be macabre —but it's my way of adapting. The purpose of a poster child is to raise interest and money in a particular cause, and I do have aspirations of doing that regarding "gay cancer."

I'm doing this for me, I'm doing this for you, and I'm doing it for our hypothetical brother standing on Castro Street who has "gay cancer" and doesn't know it. He may also be standing on Christopher Street or Santa Monica Boulevard, and he's probably not hypothetical.

I've taken to wearing a button with the title of Gloria Gaynor's 1979 hit song "I Will Survive." It seemed an appropriate title for this column. I'm writing because *I* have a determination to *live*. You do, too—don't you?

LIFE IN ALCATRAZ

CELL ISSUE EQUIPMENT

2 shelves
2 sheets stationary
2 envelopes
1 can cleanser
3 pencils
1 Radio Headset
1 sink stopper
1 75-watt light bulb
4 wall pegs
1 whisk broom
1 lamp shade
1 set institution regulations
1 roll toilet tissue
1 drinking cup
1 ash tray
2 cleaning rags
1 wastebasket

BEDDING

2 Mattresses [Max]
1 to 4 blankets
2 sheets
2 pillow cases
[if 2 pillows]
2 pillows

TOILET ARTICLES

1 shaving cup
2 razor blades
1 safety razor
1 cake soap
1 comb
1 pair nail clippers
1 can toothpowder
1 toothbrush
1 shaving brush
1 mirror

1 face towel
1 cake shaving soap

INMATES WILL BE ISSUED ON ARRIVAL:

1 B&W Pants
1 Blue shirt
1 bathrobe
1 Rain coat
1 pair slippers
1 cap and 1 belt
3 pairs socks
2 pairs shoes
1 lt undershirt
1 wool coat
1 pr shorts
2 handkerchief
1 wool undershirt
[upon request]

SUTRO BATHS

Bulletin of the Bureau of Labor, 1912

- Length of baths, 499.5 feet.
- Width of baths, 254.1 feet.
- Amount of glass used, 100,000 superficial feet.
- Iron in roof and columns, 600 tons.
- Lumber, 3,500,000 feet.
- Concrete, 270,000 cubic feet.
- Seating, amphitheater, 3,700.
- Seating promenade, 3,700.
- Holding capacity, 25,000.
- Tanks, 6.
- Capacity of tanks, 1,804,962 gallons.
- Fresh-water plunge-tank, 1.
- Toboggan slides in both, 7.
- Springboards, 9.
- Trapezes, 3.
- High Dive, 1.
- Swinging Rings, 30.
- Dressing rooms, private, 517.
- Club rooms, 9.
- Total capacity, dressing and club rooms, 1,627.
- Shower baths in all club rooms, 37.
- Shower baths in private dressing rooms, 29.
- Time required to fill tanks by waves, 1 hour.
- Time required to fill tanks by pumping, 5 hours.

FARALLON SEABIRDS

Thirty miles from the Golden Gate, this craggy, granite hinterland is the protected sanctuary for over 250,000 seabirds. (For years, a lighthouse mule also called the rocks home.) Below, 10 species of avian inhabitant.

Pigeon Guillemot .... Pitch-black plummage, white patch on wing
Tufted Puffin ....Bright-orange bill and feet, "sea parrot"
Ashy Storm Petrel................. Gray with a forked tail, disappears in the fog
Pelagic Cormorant ....Nests on cliffs, white spots if breeding
Brandt's Cormorant ....Blue eyes when breeding, hooked bill
Black Oystercatcher .... Pink legs, red bill, prefers crabs and urchins
Rhinoceros Auklet................. Growls and burrows, small "horn" by its bill
Common Murre .... Black back, long bill, pointed eggs
Marbled Murrelet ....Stumpy wings that make for good diving
California Gull......................Black wingtips, yellow bill, white underparts

GOLDEN GATE BRIDGE

Dedication Address, May 28, 1937

Imagination, genius, and courage have triumphed! The imagination of a determined group and Engineer Strauss, whose genius supplied not only a practical but a beautiful design, and the courage of these, some bankers and the Bridge District officials. From headland to headland, defining the Golden Gate, between which the "San Carlos" so proudly sailed in August, 1775, a splendid structure under which the restless waters surge and flow, first in one direction, then in the opposite, stands complete, a terrestrial glory. Its glory causes a thrill that dissipates all grief even as the sun does the morning mists which annoy from time to time as the Bridge is shut from view and the glories of the setting about it are temporarily lost to sight. This is the lay of the minstrel, Edward Rowland Sill:

I sat last night on yonder
ridge of rocks
To see the sun set over Tamalpais
Whose tinted peaks suffused
with rosy mist
Blended the colors of the sea and sky
And made the mountain
one great amethyst,
Hanging against the sun.

Man, primarily concerned with utility, has not disregarded his responsibility not to mar the beauties of nature. In the agreement with the Engineer, it was provided that he should "furnish the necessary architectural services to make the structure one of beauty and pleasing appearance to harmonize with its setting and surroundings." The Bridge blends in color and design so faithfully that it may honestly be maintained that, at least, it does not detract therefrom.

—*Francis V. Keesling*

ZODIAC KILLER

JUNE 26, 1970 This is the Zodiac speaking. I have become very upset with the people of San Fran Bay Area. They have *not* complied with my wishes for them to wear some nice [symbol] buttons. I promised to punish them if they did not comply, by anilating a full School Buss. But now school is out for the summer, so I punished them in another way. I shot a man sitting in a parked car with a .38.

LEVI'S GUARANTEE
1892

For over 20 years, our celebrated XX Blue Denim Copper Riveted Overalls have been before the public.

THIS IS A PAIR OF THEM.

They are positively superior to any made in the United States, and enjoy a national reputation. Only the very best Materials that money can purchase are used in their Manufacture.

EVERY PAIR GUARANTEED.

They are made of selected nine ounce Amoskeag denim and sewed with the strongest linen thread. We shall thank you to carefully examine the quality and fit.

By cutting the thread this ticket can be removed.

Copper Riveted Clothing Patented May 20, 1873

—Levi Strauss & Co.

HEADQUARTERS

Del Monte Foods	*Mother Jones*
Method Products	*Wired*
Square	Gap, Inc.
Esurance	Banana Republic
Charles Schwab	Levi Strauss & Co.
Kiva	Williams-Sonoma
The Sierra Club	Pottery Barn
Wikimedia Foundation	Craigslist
Airbnb	Dropbox
Kimpton Hotels	Salesforce
Dolby Laboratories	Pinterest
Lucasfilm	Yelp
Chronicle Books	Twitter
McSweeney's	BitTorrent
	OpenTable

FILM

film	famous locations
The Maltese Falcon, 1941	City overview shots, rest in L.A.
Lady from Shanghai, 1947	Funhouse at Playland at the Beach
Vertigo, 1958	Detectives on Russian Hill rooftops
The Birds, 1963	Opening scene, birds in Union Square
Bullitt, 1968	McQueen's Mustang chase scene
Dirty Harry, 1971	Ransom drop on Mount Davidson
American Graffiti, 1973	Date night at Mel's Drive-In
Big Trouble in Little China, 1986	Supernatural Chinatown brawl
Basic Instinct, 1992	Highway 1 to Stinson Beach
Sneakers, 1992	Rudy's Can't Fail Cafe
Mrs. Doubtfire, 1993	Victorian at Steiner & Broadway
So I Married an Axe Murderer, 1993	North Beach butcher, Prudente
The Rock, 1996	All parts of Alcatraz, true or not
Milk, 2008	Castro Camera shop, City Hall
The Diary of a Teenage Girl, 2015	Minnie's house in the Haight
Steve Jobs, 2015	Davies Symphony Hall
The Last Black Man in San Francisco, 2019	Fillmore District

GOLDEN DRAGON MASSACRE

The Golden Dragon Massacre, as it's called, took place between two neighborhood gangs, the Joe Boys and the Wah Ching, at odds over forbidden pyrotechnics trafficking, on September 4, 1977. Three Joe Boys gunmen entered a local restaurant on Washington Street with semiautomatics, spraying bullets across the room, killing five unsuspecting bystanders and injuring another 11 more. A $100,000 bounty was advertised by Mayor Moscone, who also reestablished the SFPD's "Chinatown Squad." By the end of October, detectives pieced together the evidence to arrest the three masked shooters, their drivers, and accomplices. After the shooting, the Golden Dragon Restaurant remained open until 2006 when finally it was forced to close due to health violations. The restaurant reopened under the name Imperial Palace, though its awning still reads "Golden Dragon Dining" so many yeas later.

SHERIFF'S CALLS

Point Reyes Light, August 2013

· OLEMA: At 3:04 p.m. a black cow was in the road.

· INVERNESS: At 8:59 p.m. someone heard a loud noise, like that of an engine.

· NICASIO: At 9:55 p.m. a woman complained about a neighbor's loud rap music.

· DILLON BEACH: At 10:09 p.m. several cows were in the road.

· WOODACRE: At 11:40 p.m. five teenagers were running down a hill, laughing.

· BOLINAS: At 1:55 p.m. a citizen concerned about nature reported that three youths with dogs had spooked seals off a sandbar. Deputies passed the information on to county rangers.

· MUIR BEACH: At 9:06 a.m. a van drove into a ditch near the Zen Center.

· POINT REYES STATION: At 10:08 a.m. someone called from Marin Sun Farms to report that animal activists had been vandalizing the business's city buildings.

· CHILENO VALLEY: At 4:24 p.m. a woman reported that her son sold her goats for $2,100 and didn't give her the money.

· WOODACRE: At 10:56 a.m. a resident complained about an elderly Prius driver who constantly speeds through the neighborhood.

SAN FRANCISCO NAVAL SHIPYARD

Weights of materials commonly handled by riggers.

Aluminum	166 lbs	Iron Casting	450 lbs
Brass	524 lbs	Lead	708 lbs
Brick [common]	120 lbs	Lumber [Fir, Spruce]	32 lbs
Bronze	534 lbs	Lumber [Oak]	62 lbs
Concrete	150 lbs	Magnesium	109 lbs
Copper	537 lbs	Mercury	848 lbs
Crushed Rock	95 lbs	Steel	490 lbs

"A TRIP TO THE CLIFF HOUSE"

By Mark Twain

The San Francisco
Daily Morning Call

June 25, 1864

If one tires of the drudgeries and scenes of the city, and would breathe the fresh air of the sea, let him take the cars and omnibuses, or, better still, a buggy and pleasant steed, and, ere the sea breeze sets in, glide out to the Cliff House. We tried it a day or two since. Out along the rail road track, by the pleasant homes of our citizens, where architecture begins to put off its swaddling clothes, and assume form and style, grace and beauty, by the neat gardens with their green shrubbery and laughing flowers, out where were once sand hills and sand-valleys, now streets and homesteads. If you would doubly enjoy pure air, first pass along by Mission Street Bridge, the Golgotha of Butcherville, and wind along through the alleys where stand the whiskey mills and grunt the piggeries of "Uncle Jim."... Then away you go over paved, or planked, or Macadamized roads, out to the cities of the dead, pass between Lone Mountain and Calvary, and make a straight due west course for the ocean. Then there's the Cliff House, perched on the very brink of the ocean, like a castle by the Rhine, with countless sea-lions rolling their unwieldy bulks on the rocks within rifle-shot, or plunging into and sculling about in the foaming waters. Steamers and sailing craft are passing, wild fowl scream, and sea-lions growl and bark, the waves roll into breakers, foam and spray, for five miles along the beach, beautiful and grand, and one feels as if at sea with no rolling motion nor sea-sickness, and the appetite is whetted by the drive and the breeze, the ocean's presence wins you into a happy frame, and you can eat one of the best dinners with the hungry relish of an ostrich. Go to the Cliff House. Go ere the winds get too fresh, and if you like, you may come back by Mountain Lake and the Presidio, overlook the Fort, and bow to the Stars and Stripes as you pass.

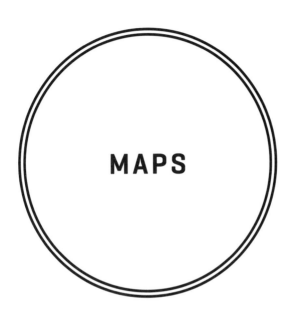

MAPS

Hand-illustrated maps to get close looks at ocean and bay,
famed architecture, Asian cuisine, urban wildlife, the history of
counterculture and where to find the best San Francisco views.

TOMALES BAY
HWY 101
HOG ISLAND OYSTER COMPANY
SAN FRANCISCO OCEAN & BAY
LANDS END
MOLLUSK SURF SHOP
GOLDEN GATE PARK
OCEAN BEACH
ROWS & ROWS OF LITTLE HOUSES
19TH AVENUE

ALIto

→ BRAR, It's COLD.

THE DOLPHIN CLUB

FERRY BLDG FARMERS MARKET

AMERICA'S CUP PAVILLION

VAN NESS AVENUE

STREET

MISSION BAY

OCEAN & BAY

*Throwback swim clubs, surfers under the bridge and floating neighborhoods:
SF locals love the water, no matter the season.*

MOLLUSK SURF SHOP

The low-key style shop is more than fancy board shorts, it's the Outer Sunset's unofficial community center, equal parts outfitter and gallery. And home to a killer treehouse by local Jay Nelson. *4500 Irving St, mollusksurfshop.com*

HOG ISLAND OYSTER COMPANY

From a five-acre shellfish lease in 1983, John Finger and Terry Sawyer found bivalve paradise in the brackish waters of Tomales Bay. It's worth the awesome 90-minute drive north to eat them fresh. *20215 Highway 1, hogislandoysters.com*

FERRY PLAZA FARMER'S MARKET

All things local, all the time. Early birds hit this Embarcadero classic at 8 a.m. on Saturday to admire California's bounty and grub on a hot breakfast by the water. *1 Ferry Bldg, cuesa.org*

THE DOLPHIN CLUB

Not for the faint of heart, club members brave frigid bay temperatures [averaging 50s F] for year-round swims. Established in 1877 by German immigrants, headstrong Dolphins refuse wetsuits and fins. *502 Jefferson St, dolphinclub.org*

MISSION CREEK HOUSEBOATS

Mission Creek has transformed from an industrial canal to a prime development zone in recent decades, but 20 floating homes continue to live a charmed life just a mile from downtown, leased through 2055.

RACING SAILS

San Francisco hosted the famed America's Cup yacht competition in 2013, creating a legacy of high-speed sailing that continues. Several regular excursions get out in competitive boats, including regatta racing under seasoned captains' tutelage. *acsailingsf.com*

OCEANIC FINDS *Saltwater explorers Kirk and Camilla Lombard lead heralded coastal tours with gusto. Ask Kirk about his California-record monkeyface eel catch. seaforager.com*

FAMOUS BUILDINGS

San Francisco's architecture fits its self-image as the Pacific Rim's queen city, and a long history of combining culture and power.

PALACE OF FINE ARTS
An otherworldly relic of the 1915 Panama-Pacific Exposition, though what we see today is the product of a 1970s rebuild. With its open rotunda and glimmering lagoon, the design evokes a fantasy riff on classical ancient ruins. *3601 Lyon St*

CLIFF HOUSE
Dating to 1909, the Golden Gate's neoclassical treasure is the third interation on a history-dense site. [The majestic 1896 version burned down in 1907, after surviving the big quake.] The onsite restaurant closed, contentiously, in 2020. *1090 Point Lobos Ave*

CASTRO THEATER
Marking its 100th anniversary in 2022, the lavish 1,400-seat movie palace mashes up international motifs. A rallying point for gay San Francisco since the '70s, home to events like the lauded Jewish Film Fest. *429 Castro St*

SENTINEL BUILDING
This emerald-green, flatiron-style beacon of culture at the crossroads of North Beach and Chinatown was once home to the famed comedy/music club hungry i. It's now homebase for filmmaker Francis Ford Coppola's creative empire and its Cafe Zoetrope. *916 Kearny St*

JAMES C. FLOOD MANSION
Nob Hill's only earthquake survivor, this silver baron's brownstone manse harks back to San Francisco's dominant position in the the early industrial West. Now home to the ultra-elite Pacific-Union Club. *1000 California St*

TRANSAMERICA PYRAMID
Flashy architect William Pereira's futurist obelisk courted controversy from drawing board to ribbon-cutting, but has symbolized urban moxie since 1972. Changed hands for $650M in 2020. *600 Montgomery St*

VICTOR VICTORIA *SF is synonymous with ornate Victorian homes, arrayed like London rowhouses but reliant on California redwood.* Painted Ladies: San Francisco's Resplendent Victorians [1978] *is the classic.*

FAMOUS BUILDINGS

CLIFF HOUSE

THE CLIFF HOUSE

JAMES C.

THE CAS
THEATR

PALACE
NE ARTS

THE TRANSAMERICA
PYRAMID

SENTINEL BUILDING

HWY 80

SION

HWY 101

SAN FRANCISCO
COUNTER CULTURE
GOLDEN
GATE PARK
HELLS ANGELS

COUNTERCULTURE

No city attracts boundary-pushers and outliers quite like San Francisco, where protestors and drag queens live together.

HARVEY MILK AND THE CASTRO

Originally a suburban Irish hood, this area became home to a thriving gay population by the 1970s, serving as ground zero for Harvey Milk's fight for LGBTQ rights and the '80s AIDS crisis. *glbthistory.org*

BALMY ALLEY

The painted alley between 24th and 25th in the Mission dates to the 1970s and the all-women activist group Mujeres Muralistas. Provocative murals, linking to Latino social consciousness, engulf unsuspecting fences and garages beneath lush bougainvillea. *balmyalley.org*

THE HUMAN BE-IN

The original "gathering of the tribes" in Golden Gate Park was the winter preface to the storied Summer of Love. The event launched the 1967 hippie all-call, championed by Jefferson Airplane, Timothy Leary, et al.

BLACK PANTHERS

Though rooted in Oakland, the Panthers ran a Fillmore Street office as an organizing hub and printing press. Here, they produced the party's famed publications, including *The Black Panther* newspaper.

THE DASH

The seediness of San Francisco's wild Barbary Coast era is brilliantly exemplified by the long-gone Dash, a notorious sex-fuelled dive once at 547 Pacfic. Cross-dressing was the norm—and this was 1908. The club lasted just six months before the vice squad swooped in.

HELL'S ANGELS

Famously reported by Hunter S. Thompson in his first published book, some of the gang's earliest clubs formed in San Francisco. As Thompson quipped, the members were "tough, mean and potentially as dangerous as a pack of wild boar."

READ ALL OVER *Before* Rolling Stone *or* Wired, *there was* Ramparts. *Originally a Catholic journal, the title became a muckraking mainstay of the '60s left. See Peter Richardson's book* A Bomb in Every Issue.

WILDLIFE

Paving the peninsula doesn't keep out Northern California's wildest animals, from parrots to sea lions to roaming coyotes.

GOLDEN GATE PARK BUFFALO

The majestic brutes first herded into Golden Gate Park in 1891 as a sort of Wild West curiosity, and now roam in a paddock near Spreckels Lake. It's an all-female line-up these days, after a few infusions of new talent over the years.

....

PARROTS ON THE STEPS

The vertiginous Filbert Steps on Telegraph Hill are the jungly perch for cherry-headed conures, made avian celebrities by Mark Pittman's tome, *The Wild Parrots of Telegraph Hill.*

....

FISHERMAN'S WHARF SEA LIONS

The lively patch of tourist kitsch along Fisherman's Wharf gives way to the floating docks of Pier 39 and the raft of sea lions who call this home, lured into the bay by a herring run in 1990.

....

SEABIRDS ON THE FARALLONS

Twenty-seven miles offshore, the craggy Farallon Islands are California's answer to the Galapagos, where at least 250,000 birds; from Cassin's auklets to tufted puffins, meet and greet.

....

COYOTES IN THE PRESIDIO

A wily population of unclear origin, these coyotes stand accused of terrorizing the Presidio. Rumors swirl that the pack was planted [!!] in 2000 to hunt feral cats and gophers.

....

TULE ELK AT POINT REYES

A once-prolific species, tule elk were reintroduced in 1978, and now occupy a large reserve off Tomales Bay. It's hard to find a more awe-inspiring Pacific trail run than this.

....

CLAUDE THE ALBINO ALLIGATOR

Born in Florida weighing only two ounces, the now-grown Claude's bad vision and errant behavior led his former tank mate, Bonnie, to nearly snap his foot off at the California Academy of Sciences.

MENAGERIE *The Animal Connection, a venerable spot just south of Golden Gate Park, serves as a pet store but also a refuge for rescued and surrendered companions.* 3401 Irving St.

SAN FRANCISCO WILDLIFE.

Pt REYES

FARALLON ISLANDS

THE PACIFIC OCEAN

ACADEMY OF SCIENCES

GOLD... PA...

CLAUDE the ALBINO ALLIG...

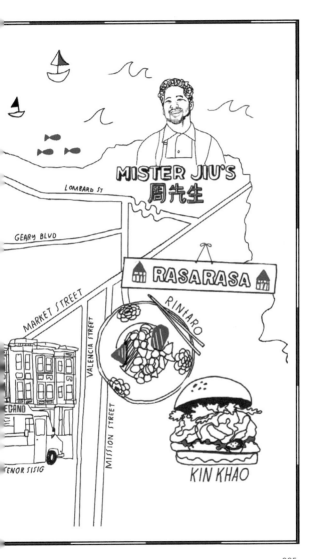

MISTER JIU'S
周先生

LOMBARD ST

GEARY BLVD

RASARASA

MARKET STREET

VALENCIA STREET

RINTARO

MISSION STREET

ECANO

ENOR SISIG

KIN KHAO

NEW ASIAN CLASSICS

San Francisco boasts many age-old Chinese and Japanese restaurants—but also a fresh wave of pan-Pacific culinary inspiration.

RINTARO

Born in Kyoto and raised in Northern California, Sylvan Mishima Brackett runs this izakaya spot with a yakitori grill and hand-rolled udon noodles. California ingredients put a local stamp on casual Japanese classics. *82 14th St*

MISTER JIU'S

This modern Cantonese restaurant has become a proving ground for chefs since it opened in 2016. Brandon Jew, a San Francisco native, revamps dishes of his youth in the iconic former Four Seas banquet hall. *28 Waverly Pl*

KIN KHAO DOGPATCH

Pim Techamuanvivit turned her focus to this outpost of her Union Square Thai restaurant during the pandemic. The fast-casual satellite serves lively dishes like a bright papaya salad and a fried chicken sandwich with coconut-cream marinade. *690 Indiana St*

JU-NI

At the counter of this intimate omakase sushi bar, featuring Michelin-starred chef Geoffrey Lee, every four diners get a personal chef to guide each course. *1335 Fulton St*

BURMA SUPERSTAR

Desmond Tan, who came to San Francisco from Burma [now Myanmar] as a child in the 1970s, has owned the Burma Superstar restaurant group for more than 20 years. The San Francisco flagship features slow-cooked mohinga and the locally famous tea leaf salad. *309 Clement St*

RASA RASA

The Southeast Asian food truck opened in Mission Bay's Parklab Gardens just before the 2020 pandemic hit. The menu specializes in Indonesian mainstays like beef rendang, gado gado, and nasi goreng and offers extensive vegan options. *1379 4th St*

BANCHAN BONANZA *Local fans of adventure-snacking and pantry stocking rejoiced at the 2021 arrival of H Mart, huge Korean grocery and food hall: 3995 Alemany Blvd.*

VISTAS

Soaring views come quick in the city of 50 hills—
street corners, park overlooks and an all-glass museum tower.

TWIN PEAKS

Second in height only to Mount Davidson, Twin Peaks [904 and 922 feet, respectively] offers the panoramic-est view of SF. Drop two quarters into the telescope for close-ups of the Transamerica and beyond.

....

TOP OF FILLMORE

Climbing from Japantown past jazz clubs and fancy shops, one reaches this bay breathtaker at the north corner of Broadway, where Fillmore takes a rollercoaster dive towards the Marina.

....

BUENA VISTA PARK

Circa 1867, San Francisco's oldest park stands atop 40 acres of hillside in the heart of the city— perfect for an afternoon hike near Haight-Ashbury.

....

IMMIGRANT POINT

High atop a cliff in the Presidio, Immigrant Point overlooks Baker Beach and the Pacific. Hike the "thousand steps" through the pines towards the waterfront bluff.

....

DE YOUNG MUSEUM

The gently spiraling, 144-foot tower design by Herzog & de Meuron in one corner of the museum offers an all-glass, 360-degree vista out over the Sunset and Richmond neighborhoods. Feels like floating.

....

BERNAL HEIGHTS HILL

At only 433 feet, the hill atop Bernal Heights still offers an unspoiled glimpse over the stunning cityscape. Plus, some serious outlaw soapbox derbies every October. Shhhh.

....

MARIN HEADLANDS

Driving over the Golden Gate, to your immediate left is the Marin Headlands—the very best view of SF, foggy or clear skies. Climb Hawk Hill with the blue butterflies to stock your IG feed with treasure.

MURK MAVEN *Fog is no doubt the nemesis of high views across the bay. To learn from the best, try Harold Gilliam's* Weather of the San Francisco Bay Region, *a fantastic [and quick] read on the city's ocean of air.*

SAN FRANCISCO VISTAS

HAWK HILL

IMMIGRANT POINT

DE YOUNG MUSEUM

TWIN PEAKS SUMMIT

INTERVIEWS

Fifteen conversations with locals of note about street art, LGBTQ
history, the city past and future, God, technology, coffee,
immigrating from China and more.

GUY CLARK

FLOWER STAND OWNER

I STARTED ON Fillmore and Haight with nine buckets. I sold all my flowers the first day. The second day, a policeman came up and said, "I love you, but you see that guy across the street at that flower shop with his arms crossed? He doesn't like you."

I'VE BEEN right on this corner in Duboce Triangle ever since, for 31 years.

I ASKED THE LADY inside that business if I could sell flowers outside their window. It was a medical lab. She said, "Oh my God, have we been waiting for you!"

SAN FRANCISCO was 13 percent Black then. Now it's less than 3 percent.

WHEN THEY BOUGHT UP all the buildings, they evicted us all, no matter if you were sick or old.

FOR TWO YEARS, I slept in my car. Parked right here.

WE CAN PUT A MAN IN SPACE, but we turn our backs on the people who really need help.

IN THE '80S, there were so many funerals in this neighborhood, it was just unbelievable. You'd see someone one day and not the next and be afraid to ask.

IT WAS TABOO. It was that thing, but no one knew what it was.

CAN YOU IMAGINE? The AIDS obituaries were page after page after page.

PEOPLE WOULD COME to me and say, "My lover died and I don't have any money and I don't know what I'm going to do." And I said, "Don't worry, we'll get them to the other side with grace and flowers."

YOU JUST HAD to have faith.

WE GIVE THEM when you're born, when you marry, when you go to heaven. Flowers are healing.

CHAD ROBERTSON

BREAD BAKER

I EAT BREAD every day.

IF I DON'T FEEL LIKE ripping off a piece and eating it, subconsciously I know there's something wrong.

WHEN I WAS IN culinary school, I went to visit a very charismatic baker in the Berkshires named Richard Bourdon. His whole place had this huge smell. I asked him on the spot if I could be his apprentice.

IN TEXAS, I didn't grow up with natural leavened bread.

AN AUSTRALIAN GUY named Alan Scott helped us build our first oven.

THE ARCHES, the height, the thickness of the walls, it was perfect. When you fired that thing and let it sit, the entire oven would become the same temperature.

A WOOD-FIRED OVEN turns black when it gets hot enough, it burns clean, burns white, and then you take the ashes out and mop it and put your bread in.

BBQ OVENS burn black. It flavors whatever you're cooking. I had a lot to learn when I left Texas.

THREE YEARS AFTER we opened Tartine, something just happened. Now, if there's not a line, people keep walking.

WE SWITCHED all our flour to fresh-milled, high-extraction grain grown in the Pacific Northwest. Pretty special stuff.

WE DON'T REALLY use white flour any more, and I wouldn't call it whole wheat. Something in between.

IN SEOUL, there's a crazy coffee and bakery culture. A lot of Western influence, but a very distinct Korean perspective on all of it. That's why we're there.

WHEN WE OPEN something new, I'm there every day for two or three months, until my team kicks me out.

REVEREND GLENDA HOPE

MINISTER

I MOVED TO San Francisco in the 1960s to go to seminary. I always planned to return to the South.

I DON'T THINK THAT any one faith has God in a box. God is much too big for that.

A GUY STRUNG OUT on drugs came to us, and we took him to the hospital. He said the next day, "I don't remember the drugs. I just remember thinking, If I can just get to you all, I'll be ok."

IF YOU'RE going to be afraid, you can't work here.

IN 40 YEARS I've only had hands laid on me in anger twice. And I'm only five feet tall and barely 100 pounds.

THE PEOPLE in the Tenderloin don't have the buffers against hardship and death. They are right there.

IN 1996, in three months, I performed five memorial services for prostituted women who were murdered. That's when we started the safe house.

HEALING comes from feeling loved.

I DON'T HEAR "Why did God do this to me?" from the people in the Tenderloin.

THEY TEND to take on too much shame.

IN 41 YEARS, I've done over 1,000 memorials.

SOME I'LL DO on the street. I put up a notice, such and such time, and people will just come.

GOD IS LOVE. God is a God of inclusive love. That is the core.

I GREW UP in Georgia, and I was unthinkingly racist and sexist and homophobic.

ALL OF THAT has been changed in me by knowing people.

I'VE BEEN set free by oppressed people. Not the other way around.

> *Learn more at sfsafehouse.org*

MAGGIE ZENG

LEVI'S MASTER SEWER

WE MOVED FROM CHINA at the end of 1983. I was 19. We lived in Richmond district.

....

MY FIRST IMPRESSION was that the city was very quiet. In China there are people everywhere. In San Francisco, there's not a lot.

....

I DIDN'T KNOW any English. Zero. Hello. Bye-bye. I love you. That's all. But I could smile.

....

I'VE ONLY been back to China once.

....

I'M THE OLDEST of my brother and sister, which is why I needed to get a job right away to take care of my family.

....

MY AUNT worked in the Levi's factory, and they trusted her, so she got me the job.

....

AT LEVI'S, I only did 501s. There were 60 women sewing, all in one room. I was the youngest, so my first job was setting the waistband.

I LEARNED in China from my neighbor. The first thing she taught me were the pants. Easy. Front panel and back panel and the elastic.

....

THE 501S are the only Levi's with a button fly. They are the first ones.

....

ONE TIME I sewed my finger with the orange thread. But only once.

....

NOW, it takes me four hours to sew a pair. Our Valencia department could do 2,000 in a day.

....

WHEN IT CLOSED, everyone was really sad. I thought I'd work there until I retired. I worked a little while in a restaurant.

....

WHEN LEVI'S opened the new factory this year, they called me. I was really excited and a little bit surprised, because I thought they'd never come back from overseas.

....

I'M THE OLDER PERSON now. It's opposite of before. The younger sewers ask me things, and I share whatever I know.

ANNALEE NEWITZ

WRITER

SAN FRANCISCO'S history really does paint the present. This was a town full of people who wanted to make money on gold or other schemes.

THERE WERE GAMBLING establishments and party venues and sex workers. This is a city founded on parties, money and sex.

YOU SEE IT again in the 1960s. That's just how we do it here.

WE FIGHT AND we party. We make weird art that often involves wearing strange goggles to have visions of robots floating through the sky.

HIGH TECH and radical artistic expression are intertwined here. There's always been this flow of money between industrial capitalism and the arts. There's also been a huge battle between them.

I REMEMBER ANTI-TECH graffiti in about 2000—beautiful stencils, lovingly crafted to tell people to fuck right off. That's a very San Francisco thing.

IN *FOUR LOST CITIES*, I write about ancient cities that had the same kinds of failure we have in our cities now. Flooding. Rampant gentrification.

I THINK ABOUT San Francisco a lot when I write about cities, partly because I love this city so much. It's really unique in so many ways. And it's also doomed.

I HAVE A poster in my hallway by a fantastic blogger who goes by Burrito Justice: San Francisco after 200 feet of sea-level rise.

JUST A BUNCH of islands. I look at that map and think, Okay, in 1,000 years my city will be an underwater archaeological site.

THAT MAKES ME feel a sense of urgency about enjoying it.

I IMAGINE WHAT will happen is, San Francisco will move inland in some sense.

I ALWAYS JUST assumed that when I grew up I would live in San Francisco.

SCOTT DADICH

DESIGNER, EDITOR, FILMMAKER

IT'S THE THINGS THAT I dislike initially that end up having the most promise over time.

YOU GET A CHURN in your belly, a little tightness in your chest. You want to look away, turn it off. All the way through the pulse rate in your ears.

THERE'S A PATCHWORK that can exist when different people with different ideas and different backgrounds and different cultures rub up against one another.

THE BEST CITIES are built on imperfection and imprecision, in a condition of metamorphosis.

LOOK DOWN the street: that block right there didn't exist before 1906. They pushed all the rubble from the earthquake down and it became landfill. You walk by a house and see twisted up bricks that were burned in the fire. They collected those and built a new house with them.

I HAVE MOSTLY lived here since 2006. The splendor of the Bay Area opened itself up: Ocean Beach and Muir Woods and the wine country. It's a bounty.

BUT LIVING HERE has been disconcerting, as well, to see the changes in neighborhoods, in lifestyle. People experiencing homelessness at a scale you just can't help but find really troubling. The gap between the haves and the have-nots.

THE TRUTH of it is that San Francisco does struggle with itself.

IT IS ABOUT listening to people. It's about research. It's about knowing how the world is working.

IT'S ABOUT understanding that curve of innovation and a human's ability to understand the way the world is changing. And that gap between those two curves is critical.

WE UNRAVEL that tension, expose it and embrace the feelings that come out of that discomfort. Maybe doing things in a different way is the more optimal path.

HALL NEWBEGIN

JUNIPER RIDGE FOUNDER

SMELL IS the most ignored of our senses, but I've always seen the world through my nose.

....

I FEEL LIKE a dog most days.

....

NATURE IS this giant book I feel like I'm always learning to read.

....

ONE PERCENT of our DNA is dedicated to smell. That's 100 times our eyesight.

....

I CAN SPEND 20 minutes on a patch of earth a foot wide.

....

PEOPLE OUT WEST tend to re-invent themselves. We're a little more cut-loose, untethered, less connected to our past. And we've always been good at being weird.

....

THE NATURAL WORLD is my church and the trail is my ritual. I don't know religious experience, but the stillness and quiet turns me into something insignficant in the face of this massive thing.

....

EVERY PARISIAN perfumer did what we do one hundred years ago. Sort of.

ENTREPRENEURS ARE often riveted by beauty. Passion and profitability are different things.

....

WE KEPT OUR story secret for a long time. We're still shy about it. But the stuff in the bottle is beautiful and real.

....

THE PACIFIC in the San Francisco air is really strong on most days. Fog and sunshine.

....

WEIRDOS CHANGE the world, even if all they do is wander the Pacific Crest Trail.

....

I STARTED Juniper Ridge in my girlfriend's apartment. I would put black sage in the blender with olive oil and press the high button. We had some hassles with her deposit.

....

THE EUREKA MOMENT was making a soap with all Big Sur plants. I took it to the bathtub with a nice big frosty pint of Lagunitas, and I was like Goddammit, I did it. This whole bathroom smells like Big Sur.

Hall Newbegin died in 2020 at the age of 52.

SHELLEY LINDGREN

SOMMELIER AND RESTAURATEUR

IF YOU ARE A SERVER in a restaurant, your wine list is your responsibility. Period.

THE WORD "BUTLER" comes from the French word for bottle opener. I love that.

THE TASTING PART of the sommelier exam is done blind. Six wines, and it's timed. You have to tell the grape, where it's from, and the vintage.

I STUDIED for four years before I took my first level.

WHEN I WAS GROWING UP north of the city, I didn't even know I was in wine country.

MY OLDEST SON has been eating sea urchin since he was two. Times change.

SONOMA COUNTY is huge. You have the east-west rivers, where pinot noir and chardonnay thrive because it's cool at night. And the valleys that go north and south, like Dry Creek, are warmer, for your Syrahs and cabernets. Those grapes love the heat.

AN ALL-ITALIAN WINE LIST in San Francisco is a risk.

WHEN WE OPENED A16, ten years ago, we knew that we always wanted it to be a place you could just drop in.

WE HAVE A PASTA DISH called maccaronara. It's a long, thick noodle from Campagna, and we serve it with a tomato ragu and house ricotta salata. That's the staple.

IT'S A COMFORT FOOD, definitely. But it takes hours to make, so having someone else make it is even better.

YOU'RE nourishing body and spirit.

ME? Sleep is something I could do better.

WHEN I'M AT WORK, I think I should be home. When I'm home, I think I should be at the restaurant. I love it all.

EMBRACE THE CHAOS.

ROB FORBES

BICYCLE DESIGNER

THE BIKE really hasn't changed that much since 1880.

THE ENGLISH are considered the first. But in a nanosecond, bikes were everywhere.

ARE YOU a Volkswagen guy or a Porsche guy? No one knows with bikes.

BIKES HAVE GOTTEN all logo-ed up, all shades of dark, geared towards dudes in their twenties.

IF WOMEN ARE RIDING on the streets, everyone else will follow.

MOST OF THE INDUSTRY is thinking about shaving a tenth of an ounce off the frame. It's driven by manufacturers.

PUBLIC BICYCLES wouldn't be in business if we didn't get the colors right. There's nothing more important.

A KICKSTAND adds weight, yes, but that's ok.

OUR FIRST COLOR was orange.

I took it right off my old Vespa.

WHITE TIRES, simple, monochromatic, a bit retro.

WE MAKE BIKES, but we think a lot about urban design too.

COPENHAGEN wasn't always a cool bike city. It was a give-and-take that went on for decades. We're just getting started in SF.

AMERICAN CITIES were designed around the automobile after WWII. Most European cities were built for the horse.

THE 1989 EARTHQUAKE completely opened up the city.

EVERY MORNING, I go out of my garage onto Hyde and turn right, careful not to get caught in cable car tracks. I wiggle through the mobs of tourists at Lombard and head down a steep hill that looks straight out over the bay, a drop-dead view.

I'M THE GUY who rides right in the middle of the lane.

ZIO ZIEGLER

ARTIST

I GOT ARRESTED in eighth grade for putting a little sticker on a stop sign. The police brought me back to my house and my parents laughed at them.

I WOULD SNEAK OUT of my house and ride my bike into the city at night on these adventures, and I got to see these amazing graffiti pieces going up and guys on rooftops.

THEY WERE LIKE superheroes with spray paint.

I THINK NAÏVE is the wrong word for it. It is raw, primitive and childlike expression of soul.

THE FIRST TIME, we wore collared shirts and just started painting a dilapidated wall. It was daytime. But no one bothered us. People were walking by asking if we needed water. They were thanking us.

WE DID A LITTLE BIT OF bullshitting too. Like, "Yeah, I'm from the San Francisco Public Beautification Committee."

SIX CANS OF Montana spray paint, gas mask, filters, a fleece, headphones, and a book on tape. I always listen to books when I paint.

I WAS PAINTING a piece on Mission. It was 60 feet tall and 150 feet long, and I was listening to *Decline and Fall of the Roman Empire*. For the tiger on Bartlett, I was listening to the fall of the Italian aristocracy.

I PROMISE I'm not always listening to the fall of something.

EVERY mistake is an opportunity.

THAT'S WHY I often do murals in one sitting.

I LIKE TO STOP PEOPLE. I like gigantism. I like beautiful, simple, pure things out in the public square.

WHEN MERCHANTS RUN the state and not the philosopher-king, we're all pretty fucked. I'm botching Plato there, but life is short and art is long.

TAL MOORE

COFFEE SOURCER

I TRAVEL 130 DAYS a year, getting to know farmers and co-ops all over the world.

THERE'S ALWAYS more to be understood. There's always new coffee that has to be roasted differently.

MY FIRST BARISTA job was at Jack's in New York City. I just couldn't sit in front of a screen anymore.

WHO KNEW that fruit flavors could come out of a coffee?

MY JOB is to find the very best green coffee at the source.

IN ETHIOPIA, I take samples from the mills and spend time late at night in a friend's lab in Addis, just tasting and tasting, looking for the most potential.

CUPPING IS basically coffee cowboy-style. A few bowls, and you pour water on grinds, evaluating the fragrance and scooping up a quick sip.

IT MIGHT BE 500 samples from one farm.

ONCE YOU LEAVE, you never know if the coffee is really going to arrive.

IF YOU'RE ALONE and you're really sick, tasting coffees is the last thing you want to do. You dream of San Francisco.

BUT WHEN a farmer kills a sheep for you or cracks open a beehive or has beer for you, and you're camping in the mountains, it's pretty special.

WE'RE GETTING coffees from Guatemala, El Salvador, Ethiopia and Kenya. All of those shipments represent a few weeks in those places and a lot of coffee tasting.

LATE SPRING to me is like Christmas.

WHEN WE ROAST, there's no computer. It's smelling and listening and looking.

CRAFT COMES from time and energy and a lot of intention.

DILSA LUGO

RESTAURANT OWNER

I'M FROM CUERNAVACA. Morelos is the state, very close to Mexico City.

I CAME TO the Bay Area in 2003 with my husband. He's a carpenter, he has this nice project. It was supposed to be for two years.

I STUDIED HORTICULTURE in Mexico. The farmers' market movement here is amazing.

WE'RE TALKING ABOUT 18 years ago. I didn't find good Mexican food.

I DIDN'T EVEN know what burritos were.

I JUST WANTED to serve things that, for real, we eat.

DO YOU KNOW tlacoyitos? It's like a small gordita in a different shape. Inside, it has requesón with epazote. We make it with blue corn masa.

YOU KNOW WHAT you want to cook, but from that point, to be a restaurant owner, it's a lot.

THE INCUBATOR La Cocina helped with basically everything. A lot of connections. I did an internship at A16, two days at Chez Panisse, then worked for a year and a half at a Mexican restaurant in Sausalito.

WE OPENED THE original Los Cilantros in Berkeley seven years ago. In Mexico, for freshness, everything's about cilantro.

THE MUNICIPAL Marketplace, if I don't have this opportunity, I will never be in San Francisco itself. For real, I wouldn't be able to pay $10,000 rent.

WHEN I HEARD about it, I said, this is not going to happen again, ever. I applied.

WHEN YOU COME in, you can feel all these different aromas. All these colors.

HERE, WHEN YOU want to do something and you ask for help, you can find it. If I need something, I will find somebody to help me.

CATHERINE BAILEY

HEATH CERAMICS OWNER

IN THE BAY AREA, people respect a crazy risk. That's the spirit of the place.

HEATH WASN'T on my radar when I moved here, even though I collected vintage pottery. It was barely chugging along.

THE FIRST PIECE I ever bought was a small-rim bowl and we used it for our cat. The cat isn't allowed to drink out of it anymore.

WHEN WE BOUGHT Heath, Robin and I walked into the same office where Edith and Brian Heath had worked for 60 years. The desk drawers were full of her stuff. Same telephone, same typewriter, same everything.

THAT'S HOW I got to know Edith.

OUR TURNING POINT was the open-book policy. Anybody in the company could see our numbers. It creates a new trust.

IT'S WAY BEYOND color and glaze. That character comes from oxides and stains, and every time you change the ingredients, it changes the piece.

WHEN YOU GO TO IKEA, you see sameness.

THE HEATH STUDIO MUG is an icon. It was designed in 1947 with a low handle that I've never seen anywhere else.

YOU ONLY GET that kind of character if you do the work.

THERE'S A CONTRAST now between super-tech and makers, but it works here.

PEOPLE WHO SIT at screens all day love to see something that's handmade.

THE COMPANY SQUARE just bought a huge new building and all their dinnerware in the cafeteria is Heath. It's the biggest order we've ever done.

WE LOOK BACK at what people loved about Heath in 1959 and try to build from there.

SIDNEY HOLLISTER

SWIM CLUB MEMBER

I JOINED the Dolphin Club 26 years ago.

ONCE IT GETS under 60 degrees in the bay, the endorphins last a lot longer. You just feel wonderful. Nothing bothers you.

THAT LONG PERIOD and the distance puts you into a meditative place that you just can't go into when you're in lap pool.

YOU LOOK UP and just see sky. It's amazing.

GO IN and don't get out for at least five minutes. It's self-selection.

SEALS ARE VERY SOCIAL. They like playing with bubbles around your feet. If you kick, they'll be right behind you.

WHEN THE SARDINES used to come in, they came by the billions. Brown pelicans dove down 30 feet. You would hear something and there would be a pelican 10 feet away, sitting on the water, eating.

THE SOUTH END CLUB? Yeah, we have a triathlon rivalry with them. They almost always win.

THE DOLPHIN CLUB started in 1877.

IT WAS MOSTLY ROWING then because the bay was filthy. A smelting factory was next door and fishing boats emptied their toilets near the wharf.

IT COST THREE BUCKS a month 30 years ago. And until 1977, women weren't allowed. They'd swim in off the beach.

YOU CAN BE ANYBODY in here. I don't know if I'd still be in this city if it weren't for this club.

THIS GUY NAMED George next door at the South End Club, a real character, he had all sorts of heart problems. Doctor said, "Don't swim in cold water anymore." But it's an addiction. So he swam and he came in and dropped dead in front of his locker.

COULD YOU ASK for anything better? I should be so lucky.

MARK SAWCHUK

HISTORIAN

I DON'T THINK it's a coincidence that America's three great queer cities are all ports. New Orleans, New York, San Francisco.

DURING THE gold rush there were 12 men to one woman, a very homosocial environment.

IT WOULD HAVE helped a young me a lot to have known about people like Phyllis Lyon and Harvey Milk.

I WAS TRANSITIONING out of academia, working on my own projects. I came across the GLBT Historical Society.

ARCHIVES—YOU HAVE TO be creative. Here are three haystacks. You know there's a needle in one of them.

THE DON LUCAS Papers document the Mattachine Society, the first major gay-rights organization in the United States.

THERE ARE LETTERS from people all over the world. One from a closeted professor at the Sorbonne in France, saying, "I get your Mattachine newspaper and newsletter." Explaining why it was important for him, in this very staid academic atmosphere in Paris.

PIECES OF PAPER. Tickets, flyers, souvenirs, stubs, matchbooks. Used once and then tossed. Generally, they don't survive.

IT TOOK ON a new valence during the AIDS epidemic. As people died, their possessions were thrown out. Their heirs didn't want them. There was a real chance of history being literally thrown out.

WE HAVE EPHEMERA from the Russian River—Guerneville in the late '70s and early '80s.

I FOUND THIS one flyer that was just brilliant. It had an image of some very campy woman, like a vampire kind of woman. And it said, "Girls, why fight it?"

SAN FRANCISCO FEELS a little like Prague. Sui generis. It doesn't exist anywhere else.

STORIES

_____

*Essays, poetry and selected writing
from noted San Francisco voices*

THE MOUNTAINS

Written by **GEORGE McCALMAN** | **"I'M COMING BACK** with you to California. I want to go to the mountains." My mother said that to me in our second conversation after her diagnosis. She was musing about her future plans, the things that she intended to do in her five months of remaining life.

I wasn't surprised; my mother was a planner. She had executed a kind of success that you hear about in documentaries: a case study of the American Dream. She had worked hard, she had saved her money, she had secured her financial foundation. It had emboldened her to plan her imminent death to pancreatic cancer, and California was one of the places she felt most like herself. Her doctor had told her "go out and live" [a terrible thing, in retrospect, for someone to say to another they know is dying], and she was only defining her intentions to meet this final edge. Same as she has always done.

I remember listening to her plan to travel with me back to the place that she had fallen in love with. My mother spoke in measured, reserved tones in her daily life, but the pitch in her melodic voice always betrayed her emotions. Anyone knew when she was excited about something. Travel excited her. Walking excited her. Nature excited her. She had found peace in the convergence of California's land, sea and air. It called her and she responded. It formed a slow but steady bridge as we attempted to heal the rift between us.

My mother and I had been estranged in some form or another since my early adulthood. Almost 30 years of silent resentments had formed a scab we could only pick at, leaving a deeper mark. We both knew the reasons, but neither of us could crest the ridge. I moved to San Francisco from New York to escape. I wanted some peace from the continual load of an unresolved rancor. I found that peace in the place that was in between.

It was years before I could articulate to myself why I had moved to a place where I knew no one and nothing, a place that felt like home almost immediately. How to explain why it did. A city that has a dwindling Black population. A place that culturally feels as far away from my Caribbean lineage as possible. A place that births industries that threaten the organic messiness of human connection with dishonest digital metrics. It was the mountains. The sea. The land. The land that still feels pure and unburdened. A counterbalance to urban strife. The place of the openness of ocean vistas. A place to find yourself in nature. The convergence of soil and trees and air and fog. I felt a silent calling. So I came to the place that was in between. In between the petite island, Grenada, that I was born to. And the grand city, New York, that I was raised in.

There was a turning point in our struggles. Annually, she would come out to California to visit. It ended the way all her trips did: with bitter animosity. We unloaded our pain and hurled it at each other as she was leaving. Our words slashed each other's hearts. We barely spoke for months afterwards. We continued to tend to our wounds separately. And then we would begin again. That was our cycle. But this time was different. My father had died. I was in pain that was separate from hers. My parents had not communicated with each other since I was 10. There was no reason for them to. When he died, it opened an awareness of how much I had been keeping from her. I was the convergence between them. I hadn't just been separated from her. I was separated from my parents. I had grown up isolated from the people who made me. But I had found myself in California. She flew out to be with me as I tended to my heartbreak. It was her first understanding that I hadn't been angry with her. I was angry with myself. I had taken responsibility for being abandoned by both of my parents.

In the month that she spent with me, we toured the land together, on urban and beach and trail walks. I told her what being in San Francisco had meant to me. How it had healed my soul. How I had discovered a deeper connection to myself. She listened to me for what felt like the first time. I remember her saying something that she had innumerable times. She likes to go to the water's edge. But she rarely went into the ocean. It was meditative, she said. It calmed her soul. I listened to her for what felt like the first time.

For many years, I had a Sunday routine. I would take the North Judah Muni train out to Ocean Beach. I would walk the entire expanse of the beach in an afternoon. It was usually in solitude. It was usually in silence. A few years ago, I rented an art studio by that same beach. It became less of a tender escape and more of a way of being. A way to meet the convergence of land, sea and fog.

"I want to go to the mountain." I laughed when she said that, and she knew it wasn't at her expense. I was happy that she was so dynamic in the face of death. I told her that I was going to go with her, and we would walk the trails of Mount Tamalpais together. When I arrived at her home in Florida to become one of her caregivers, I knew she had less time than her doctors had decreed. I knew she wouldn't be able to go to California. She knew it too.

My mother died the day after Mother's Day. I had returned to California for a few days prior to gather my things to go back to her side. But I had another reason. I walked the trails, I felt my toes in the sand of Ocean Beach. I inhaled the fog. I brought back California with me. I told her this on her deathbed. I brought the mountains back with me.

GEORGE MCCALMAN is an artist and creative director. His studio, McCalman.Co, designs brands for a range of cultural clientele. He's a visual columnist for the *San Francisco Chronicle*, featured in "Observed" and "First Person," and his first book, *Illustrated Black History*, is due to be published by Amistad/HarperCollins in 2022.

OYE COMO VA

Written by **CHRIS COLIN** | **YOU TRY TO THINK OF YOURSELF** as worldly and urban, but then a squat, balding man at the bus stop toting a bag of bright new socks and t-shirts is ticking off cities where he got laid—Copenhagen, Madrid, London, Rome—then crying in a woman's voice, high-pitched actual boo-hoos, a grown man, then he's dabbing at his eyes and resuming the inventory—Amsterdam, Paris, Athens—and your worldliness deflates, and you're just a suburban boob in the big, weird city again.

"Do you know who I am?" he was asking. We were on the corner of 24th and Mission. The insane and dissolute stumble about there in such numbers that it can take three light cycles just to inch your car across the intersection. But even with all the crazies, this fellow stood out. He turned to a woman holding a baby. "Do you know who I am?" He turned to a sullen teen. "Do you know?" They began to back away.

"I know who you are."

He turned to me. His face was droopy and soft, and sort of female, though I gathered it had seen a hard and excessively masculine period.

"Who am I?" he said, fixing his button eyes on mine.

"You're Chepito Areas."

There are ways to talk about San Francisco without talking about this fellow, but I don't know them. Partly this is climatological—our encounter fell on the one of those pale, thoughtful summer afternoons that make you think about the city itself. Something invisible in the atmosphere signals that the beers and burritos and late-night bike rides of summer are finished. Tomorrow your drafty old Victorian will feel draftier, its hallway longer and gloomier, and you'll dig out your sweaters and start making soup, and in weeks the rains will start.

So it was a ruminative day, and per city ordinance every San Franciscan was ruminating about his or her arrival here, however many months or decades back. The citizenry is entirely imported, after all—flown in from loveless Midwest clans and suffocating East Coast burgs; a radiant surfer-deity greets them on the tarmac with a margarita from Zeitgeist, and in a week their hair has grown six inches. Technically, some San Franciscans are native. But only a dozen or so, and they're always slinking off together to lament some beloved old bead shop or something. The imported San Franciscans are up on the roof, dramatically hurling their old truths over the side, plus learning to discuss coffee.

Back to the bus stop, where something about the crying and the getting laid had rung a bell. My wife, weirdly, had encountered an almost identical scene some months back, and we have the kind of relationship where you report whether or not you saw any weeping braggarts that day. I had googled the story she relayed and it checked out: Chepito Areas played percussion in Santana from 1969 to 1980. Dude played at Woodstock, was inducted into the Rock and Roll Hall of Fame. Something seemed to have happened between then and now. He had his bag of socks and t-shirts. It didn't seem like there was much else.

But I'd spoken his name and suddenly his tears vanished. His strangely waxy face pulled into a waxy smile. Immediately I was taken under his wing, which for journalism's sake, I will say smelled pretty gnarly.

"Stand here," he whisper-commanded me as our bus pulled up. "I show you how to ride free. I know the secret."

The secret is, you don't pay. We snuck on and took two seats. The butt-concavity of San Francisco MUNI seats is such that you slide into greater intimacy with your neighbor than you might prefer. Areas preferred it fine. With considerable swagger he draped a stiff drunkard's arm around my shoulders.

"See?" Areas said, nodding to the bus driver. "He knows me. Respect. Respect."

For the next ten minutes, San Francisco's Mission District lurched by alongside a jumbled and intermittently emotional narration. Areas was a legend, I was informed. Carlos Santana was a crook and a filthy one—used to sleep in the park. Stole everyone's money. Now his woman had stolen his.

Areas halted his emotional narrative if local trivia required it. We passed a ratty blue Victorian at 25th Street. Very haunted, he warned me.

Back to Santana, who's broke now, he said, living in a hotel in Vegas. He wants to get the band back together to make some scratch. Areas had a stroke in '71, he added, can't remember anything.

The city felt peaceful in its nostalgic afternoon light, but everything brought Areas anxiety. I still didn't see what all the crying was about. Then he pointed at a hill in the distance. Did I see that? I did. That hill? Yes. Did I see how big it was? I did. I used to live on a bigger one. Twin Peaks. View of whole city. Now I live by the projects. More tears. I used to drive a Rolls Royce but now look at me, riding the bus with these people. Boo-hoo. Boooo-hoooo.

He pulled himself together. Kate Middleton and Prince William's new baby? He knew it would be a boy.

It was 15 summers earlier that I'd washed up in San Francisco. I arrived with the uncomfortably fancy duffel bag a relative had given me, which didn't quite comport with the idea of washing up. I reeked of East Coast uptightness. But the scent comes off. I converted instantly and thoroughly. Everything I saw amazed me, and filled me with a strange and wooly pride. When one freeway overpass rose particularly high over another, I felt proud. When a bright green hill popped up out of nowhere, something verging on hubris welled up, as though we'd planned this hill together. Everything was in bounds. Get a load of this burrito, able to prop a door open. But my vision of San Francisco didn't really cohere until Halloween.

It was a balmy night, and some friends had dragged me to the massive party in the Castro, an annual surge of revelers that would reach 500,000 at its peak. My costume involved some ill-advised Quaker/earthquake pun. We walked up Market Street, broad and streamer-strewn. Suddenly a dozen men and women two decades our senior were all around us. They were dressed in identical jumpsuits and carried some architecturally complex structure over us. Wearing expressions of great seriousness, they shimmied and swirled their hands all over us. They were a carwash, a middle-aged carwash. No way they spent less than three weeks creating and rehearsing this thing. We passed through and watched as they walked their elaborate selves east down Market, toward their next quarry. I stared until they were out of sight.

I had never seen adults having fun. I didn't know that was a thing. I'd grown up in straight-laced Northern Virginia, a suburb of straight-laced Washington. Nobody over 18 was building elaborate anythings, not out of whimsy anyway. For fun grown-ups drove to a restaurant, then went home and paid the sitter.

The car wash thing blew my mind. Fun and spirit and *living* had no expiration date out here. What other rules were breakable? Maybe, say, all of them? The budding tech revolution obscured a deeper ontological one: Life itself had new terms. You can open an experimental theater, your rooftop farm *will* sustain, you *should* keep dropping acid. On the curvy cliff-hanging roads south of town I was astonished to encounter stretches without guardrail. Sail over if you want. Whatever.

Some do sail over.

You don't meet them at first. In the beginning it's just the upward trajectories you notice. Here is a woman who quit her job to invent toys and it's working. Here is a couple that takes their baths out in the yard and it's working. The artisanal knife sharpener is making it. The young pot-dealing church organist is making it. You mistake ascent for the absence of gravity.

Maybe the people drawn to the West are those naturally inclined toward faith. When I was nine, my friend Erik told me some kid named Peter had a Flying Elephant in his garage. What's a Flying Elephant? I asked. *You sit on it and flap it and it lifts off the ground.* What? If this Peter had such a device, how come we'd never hung out with him before? But when I went up the kid's cul-de-sac, Peter was in his garage, sitting on a garden-variety scooter. This was the Flying Elephant. Erik laughed. I was crestfallen. The point is, I was nine, not four. I knew better. But I'd wanted to believe.

A couple years after that Halloween night in the Castro, I read some book of John McPhee's in which he referred to San Francisco as "the white city." It stayed with me. I don't know why—maybe the ease with which he captured the look of the place from a distance: little white cubes at varying elevations. Maybe I sensed he was alluding to something bigger—the privilege and self-regard. Maybe I just liked that a famous writer took the time to notice my town and label it. Years later I'd looked up the phrase, wanting to find its exact provenance. Turns out every other city in the country has been called "the white city" at some point.

San Francisco has, of course, always hosted those who would defy gravity. The Gold Rush was that. The Beats were that. The Summer of Love was that. The dot-commers were that. Unbound to the earth, the Ginsbergs and Twains and Joplins and Keseys and Milks floated up into lives inconceivable elsewhere. But stay long enough and you start to notice the descents, too. The landscape is littered with fallen stars; their revivals and failings and revivals and failings merge with the architecture. You meet a Chepito Areas every couple years. They scrawl their phone numbers into your notepad on a long, odd bus ride through the Mission. You carry it around a while, always a hairsbreadth away from calling, but what is there to say?

"If I see a ghost, I have a heart attack," Areas was telling me, in the casually informative way you'd mention that your hands itch if you eat avocados. But then he went dark again. The bus crossed Cesar Chavez and groaned up Bernal Hill, where Sandinista sympathizers used to train, and where the SLA kept a safe house during the Patty Hearst kidnapping. History for Areas was a fog. Where's his money? Where's his old life? How had he fallen so far? Down the other side of the hill we went. I wake at four each morning, he told me. You must have an early bedtime, I said, trying to keep things light. Six o'clock, he said. He looked down at his watch. 6:02. That's all it took. *Booo-hoooo.*

I still think of that carwash costume occasionally. It must sound unimpressive on the page. But I swear it was something. I wonder about the people who made it—whether the city remained white and bright for them, whether it continued to feed them whatever kindling they were burning that night. The Castro's Halloween party, for its part, burned too bright. The good times turned bad and some violence in 2006 shuttered the decades-old tradition permanently.

To spend time in San Francisco isn't, of course, to live without gravity. It's to stretch a tape measure each day between that fantasy and the mundane reality that unspools every morning after breakfast. The special and poignant feelings that come out on pale and thoughtful summer afternoons, they're a product of all that tape-measuring.

Areas got off the bus sniffling and dabbing, but at the last moment he turned and seemed to brighten. The shopping bag he'd been carrying—he looked down at it and grinned. It was a silly but flickeringly sober grin. Five hundred dollars worth of *shoes and socks*, he declared.

CHRIS COLIN is the author, most recently, of *Off*, published in 2021. He's written for *The New York Times Magazine*, *Wired*, *Smithsonian*, *Mother Jones*, Pop-Up Magazine, *Afar* and more.

I ONCE THOUGHT ALL SUNSETS WERE OVER WATER

Written by **SHELLEY WONG**

Another life in the Bay & still I fall for that sunshine
ice wind. Wind that floods my silk skirt

as I whisper *eucalyptus*, my imagined safeword.
I'm a tan fourth-generation Californian

wearing socks in July. I want the Chinese grandmas
to help me pick the peaches sweet enough

for devouring. When the cashier
calls me *miss*, I'm flattered, but also

I have earned my *ma'am* respect. Old enough
& I sing of BTS—praise the one wearing a shirt

splashed with Dorothy asleep
in the Technicolor field, the poppies

overbright like lanterns. Over a hundred
years ago, my great-grandfathers refused to die

as bachelors. They found wives
in the Chinatown mission rescue homes

or brought them back from China,
sailing on the ocean's indifference

before interrogation at Angel Island.
As a living miracle: I float, curving

through a church on rollerskates,
disco-lit. I flirt & flee in ecstatic florals

across this earthquake land. Maybe I'm
the foolish future, ignoring swipe right

notifications across the gender spectrum
in another faded summer of free love,

wandering through the fog of lost parachuters,
fog of abandon, fog of broken spells—

SHELLEY WONG is the author of *As She Appears* [YesYes Books, 2022] and winner of the 2019 Pamet River Prize. Her poems have appeared in *American Poetry Review*, *Best American Poetry 2021*, *Kenyon Review* and *The New Republic*. She has received a Pushcart Prize and fellowships from Kundiman, MacDowell and Vermont Studio Center.

THE FOG CHASERS

Written by **AUGUST KLEINZAHLER**

Cold steamy air blew in through the open windows, bringing with it half a dozen times a minute the Alcatraz foghorn's dull moaning. A tinny alarm-clock insecurely mounted on a corner of Duke's Celebrated Criminal Cases of America—*face down on the table—held its hands at five minutes past two.* —Dashiell Hammett, *The Maltese Falcon*

THE NEIGHBOR WITH THE BAD DOG fiddles with her helmet and adjusts her front bicycle light before pushing off downhill in the fog. It is late for a bicycle ride, after 10 p.m. Her dog throws himself against the glass of the front window behind the curtain, nearly strangling himself with snarls and a torturous medley of barks. She is headed west, in the direction of the ocean or park. There are dangers to be found this time of night in both places. But she is a fog chaser, and deepening night is best with the wind up and the cold, damp smoke blowing in off the sea at 20 knots. I can spot them, fog chasers, after so many years here. You might even say I'm such a one myself from time to time, especially when I find myself feeling more than a little remote from "society."

In the daylight hours, walking her vicious companion, occasionally bending over to pick up its stool with a small, white, plastic baggie, one can see it in her eyes—the eyes of a fog chaser—haunted, darting about as if pursued by some threatening inner phantasm. She will rarely, if ever, engage the eyes of any stranger walking past, even as her creature takes a murderous lunge in his direction, gargling delirium at the end of his leash. But not mine—my eyes she will always look directly into, appraisingly and with a sneering displeasure. She knows that I know.

She had seen it at a matinee towards the end of her last summer in Charleston, late July, before moving west to San Francisco. To escape the terrible heat and humidity, and just escape, she'd been attending quite a few matinees in that air-conditioned multiplex, those couple of weeks after she'd quit her job and before heading out.

We were standing at the bus stop, just across from what was then the Rock & Bowl at the foot of Haight Street, just 20 yards or so from the park, across Stanyan. It was late August, mid-afternoon. We could see the fog blowing in the way it does, along the ridge to the south of us, across Twin Peaks, Tank Hill and the Sutro Forest behind the medical center.

She trembled. "You're cold," I said, wanting to put my arm around her but hesitating. We had only recently met, almost immediately after she arrived here by car, a long drive west with a friend. She was still rattled by it all: the drive, the breakup, the mess left behind—most everything, really. Presently, we would become lovers but not quite yet.

"No," she said, pausing a few moments. "I'm frightened." "Frightened?" I asked. "By what?"

She seemed loath to say, embarrassed, I suppose. We said nothing for a minute or two. Then she said, "The fog." I was puzzled, taken aback, really, but didn't reply. Again she was quiet for some time. "You know, *The Fog*, that horror movie. I saw it back in Charleston at the matinee right before I left."

"What happens with the fog in that movie?" I asked.

"Nothing good," she said, turning to look me in the eyes, now clearly frightened and drawing close. "Nothing good."

It's way out there on the avenues, the north side of the park on Balboa, maybe a mile in from the ocean, hardly any other shops around, maybe a tiny corner store or acupuncturist in the vicinity. It's a tiny place, with a big red sign above the glass front, *Shanghai Dumpling King*, with Chinese characters festooned all around the English like an aviary of tiny exotic birds.

It's bleak out there on the avenues this time of year, and gets bleaker still the closer you get to the water, and blowing. Nobody out on the street that doesn't have to be. There is a bus line runs along here but only seldom. It's not a good part of town to be waiting for the bus, not the back end of summer, I can tell you. You could compose half a sonnet sequence about the fog and wind and cold in your head while waiting for one to come by; that is if you're not stuck living out here in this godforsaken part of town and happen to know the schedule by heart.

The windows of the restaurant are fogged up by the steam, either

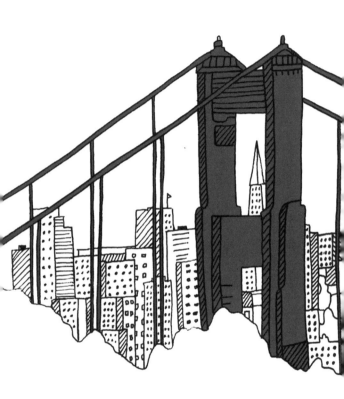

side of the glass. It's very quiet out there on the avenues, except for the low roar of wind, but inside the restaurant is all noisy plate clatter, talk, busyness. It's always jam-packed.

Do you remember those warm spring twilights back East, playing Little League, the smell of hickory or white ash, cowhide, grass, your cotton flannel uniform, stands filled, and you coming to bat against Kenny Ray, the most feared pitcher in the league, big as a grown man and mean as hell, looking down at you from the mound with menace and contempt, the catcher behind you chattering away, saying nothing very encouraging? And somehow you get the head of your Louisville Slugger, the sweet spot, smack dab right on Kenny's fastball and drive it deep, deep to right center, all the way to the the foot of the cyclone fence, deepest part of the outfield, crowd screaming, dugout screaming, Kenny looking like he just might jump right off the mound there and start chasing you down as you run the bases, probably throttle you to death.

Well, that's how they taste, the *xiaolongbao*, those Shanghai soup dumplings, when you bite into one of those plaited little darlin's, nippled at the top, the steamy-hot broth inside spurting into your mouth, bringing along with it the flavor of the pork, shrimp and chives stuffed inside. And then you know, for sure, for dead absolute certain, that in this cold, remorseless, fog-obliterated, windblown wretched old world that somewhere out there, close on by the ocean, and if you know how to find it, there *is* this, *this*.

Steam rises from the wooden cistern. He unwraps the towels from my feet and begins digging deep into the tissue of my instep, working the adrenals, duodenum and hepatic flexurs. It is near the end of the day, Sunday, and the end of a long week. The fog, which had never once burned off over the course of the day as it sometimes does this time of year, if only for an hour or two, has begun thickening, the Big Smoke Machine out there on the Pacific switching on as it always does at this hour, blowing in reinforcements down the flat, shop-lined corridor of Geary Boulevard.

There is some pain, occasionally sharp, as he probes deeper and deeper, exploring what time, misuse and neglect have wrought upon my inner organs. He says nothing, and never looks up from his ministrations, grave-faced, in total concentration, emitting only very occasionally a muffled sound that rises from the base of his throat, suggesting perhaps some grim revelation, one best left unnamed and unspoken.

Presently, he moves to my toes, pinching and pulling, raising—in his mind's eye—something like a primitive MRI or CAT scan image of my pineal, hypothalamus and axillary lymphatics. But the pain he studiously inflicts, while holding fast to the methodical regimen and sequencing of his ancient art, is never, not at any single moment, entirely divorced from acute pleasure.

The bars have emptied, or begun emptying, today's ballgame having recently concluded or the outcome inevitable. It is early yet for the restaurants, but in some of the Chinese places families have already begun gathering for their early repast, and in others the kitchen staffs, likewise, sit around large tables and grab a quick meal before the dinner rush begins. The street is largely empty now. It is an in-between time, one of several in the course of the day, and when one turns a corner from one of the side streets onto Geary at this particular hour, the wind abruptly meets you and pushes you backward as if a stern rebuke to never entirely let slip from your mind the record of all of history's misfortunes.

AUGUST KLEINZAHLER is the author of 10 books of poetry, including *The Strange Hours Travelers Keep* and *Sleeping It Off in Rapid City*. Allen Ginsberg called his work "always precise, concrete, intelligent, and rare." Kleinzahler has won a Guggenheim Fellowship, a Berlin Prize and a National Book Critics Circle Award for Poetry.

SLOUCHING TOWARDS BETHLEHEM

Written by **JOAN DIDION**

THE CENTER WAS NOT HOLDING. It was a country of bankruptcy notices and public-auction notices and commonplace reports of casual killings and misplaced children and abandoned homes and vandals who misplaced even the four-letter words they scrawled. It was a country in which families routinely disappeared, trailing bad checks and repossession papers. Adolescents drifted from city to torn city, sloughing off both the past and the future as snakes shed their skins, children who were never taught and would never now learn the games that had held society together. People were missing. Children were missing. Parents were missing. Those left behind filed desultory missing persons reports, then moved on themselves.

It was not a country in open revolution. It was not a country under enemy siege. It was the United States of America in the cold late spring of 1967, and the market was steady and the G.N.P. high and a great many articulate people seemed to have a sense of high social purpose and it might have been a spring of brave hopes and national promise, but it was not, and more and more people had the uneasy apprehension that it was not. All that seemed clear was that at some point we had aborted ourselves and butchered the job, and because nothing else seemed so relevant I decided to go to San Francisco. San Francisco was where the social hemorrhaging was showing up. San Francisco was where the missing children were gathering and calling themselves "hippies." When I first went to San Francisco in that cold late spring of 1967 I did not even know what I wanted to find out, and so I just stayed around awhile, and made a few friends.

A sign on Haight Street, San Francisco:

Last Easter Day
My Christopher Robin wandered away.

He called April 10th
But he hasn't called since
He said he was coming home
But he hasn't shown.
If you see him on Haight
Please tell him not to wait
I need him now
I don't care how
If he needs the bread
I'll send it ahead.
If there's hope
Please write me a note
If he's still there
Tell him how much I care
Where he's at I need to know
For I really love him so!

Deeply,
Marla

Marla Pence
12702 NE. Multnomah
Portland, Ore. 97230
503/252-2720.

I am looking for somebody called Deadeye and I hear he is on the Street this afternoon doing a little business, so I keep an eye out for him and pretend to read the signs in the Psychedelic Shop on Haight Street when a kid, sixteen, seventeen, comes in and sits on the floor beside me.

"What are you looking for," he says.

I say nothing much.

"I been out of my mind for three days," he says. He tells me he's been shooting crystal, which I already pretty much know because he does not bother to keep his sleeves rolled down over the needle tracks. He came up from Los Angeles some number of weeks ago, he doesn't remember what number, and now he'll take off for New York, if he can find a ride. I show him a sign offering a ride to Chicago. He wonders where Chicago is. I ask where he comes from. "Here," he says. I mean before here. "San Jose. Chula Vista, I dunno. My mother's in Chula Vista."

A few days later I run into him in Golden Gate Park when the Grateful Dead are playing. I ask if he found a ride to New York. "I hear New York's a bummer," he says.

Deadeye never showed up that day on the Street, and somebody says maybe I can find him at his place. It is three o'clock and Deadeye is in bed. Somebody else is asleep on the living-room couch, and a girl is sleeping on the floor beneath a poster of Allen Ginsberg, and there are a couple of girls in pajamas making instant coffee. One of the girls introduces me to the friend on the couch, who extends one arm but does not get up because he is naked. Deadeye and I have a mutual acquaintance, but he does not mention his name in front of the others. "The man you talked to," he says, or "that man I was referring to earlier." The man is a cop.

The room is overheated and the girl on the floor is sick. Deadeye says she has been sleeping for twenty-four hours now. "Lemme ask you something," he says. "You want some grass?" I say I have to be moving on. "You want it," Deadeye says, "it's yours." Deadeye used to be an Angel around Los Angeles but that was a few years ago. "Right now," he says, "I'm trying to set up this groovy religious group—'Teenage Evangelism.'"

Don and Max want to go out to dinner but Don is only eating macrobiotic so we end up in Japantown again. Max is telling me how he lives free of all the old middle-class Freudian hang-ups. "I've had this old lady for a couple of months now, maybe she makes something special for my dinner and I come in three days late and tell her I've been balling some other chick, well, maybe she shouts a little but then I say 'That's me, baby,' and she laughs and says 'That's you, Max.'" Max says it works both ways. "I mean if she comes in and tells me she wants to ball Don, maybe, I say 'O.K., baby, it's your trip.'"

Max sees his life as a triumph over "don'ts." Among the don'ts he had done before he was twenty-one were peyote, alcohol, mescaline, and Methedrine. He was on a Meth trip for three years in New York and Tangier before he found acid. He first tried peyote when he was in an Arkansas boys' school and got down to the Gulf and met "an Indian kid who was doing a don't. Then every weekend I could get loose I'd hitchhike seven hundred miles to Brownsville, Texas, so I could cop peyote. Peyote went for thirty cents a button down in Brownsville on the street." Max dropped in and out of most of the schools and fashionable clinics in the eastern half of America, his standard technique for dealing with boredom being to leave. Example: Max was in a hospital in New York and "the night nurse was a groovy spade, and in the afternoon for therapy there was a chick from Israel who was interesting, but there was nothing much to do in the morning, so I left."

We drink some more green tea and talk about going up to Malakoff Diggings in Nevada County because some people are starting a commune there and Max thinks it would be a groove to take acid in the diggings. He says maybe we could go next week, or the week after, or anyway sometime before his case comes up. Almost everybody I meet in San Francisco has to go to court at some point in the middle future. I never ask why.

I am still interested in how Max got rid of his middle-class Freudian hang-ups and I ask if he is now completely free.

"Nah," he says. "I got acid."

Max drops a 250- or 350-microgram tab every six or seven days.

Max and Don share a joint in the car and we go over to North Beach to find out if Otto, who has a temporary job there, wants to go to Malakoff Diggings. Otto is pitching some electronics engineers. The engineers view our arrival with some interest, maybe, I think, because Max is wearing bells and an Indian headband. Max has a low tolerance for straight engineers and their Freudian hang-ups. "Look at 'em," he says. "They're always yelling 'queer' and then they come sneaking down to the Haight-Ashbury trying to get the hippie chick because she fucks."

We do not get around to asking Otto about Malakoff Diggings because he wants to tell me about a fourteen-year-old he knows who got busted in the Park the other day. She was just walking through the Park, he says, minding her own, carrying her schoolbooks, when the cops took her in and booked her and gave her a pelvic. "*Fourteen years old*," Otto says. "A *pelvic*."

"Coming down from acid," he adds, "that could be a real bad trip."

I call Otto the next afternoon to see if he can reach the fourteen-year-old. It turns out she is tied up with rehearsals for her junior-high-school play,

The Wizard of Oz. "Yellow-brick-road time," Otto says. Otto was sick all day. He thinks it was some cocaine-and-wheat somebody gave him.

There are always little girls around rock groups—the same little girls who used to hang around saxophone players, girls who live on the celebrity and power and sex a band projects when it plays—and there are three of them out here this afternoon in Sausalito where the Grateful Dead rehearse. They are all pretty and two of them still have baby fat and one of them dances by herself with her eyes closed.

I ask a couple of the girls what they do.

"I just kind of come out here a lot," one of them says.

"I just sort of know the Dead," the other says.

MAX IS TELLING ME HOW HE LIVES FREE OF ALL THE OLD MIDDLE-CLASS FREUDIAN HANG-UPS.

The one who just sort of knows the Dead starts cutting a loaf of French bread on the piano bench. The boys take a break and one of them talks about playing the Los Angeles Cheetah, which is in the old Aragon Ballroom. "We were up there drinking beer where Lawrence Welk used to sit," Jerry Garcia says.

The little girl who was dancing by herself giggles. "Too much," she says softly. Her eyes are still closed.

Somebody said that if I was going to meet some runaways I better pick up a few hamburgers and Cokes on the way, so I did, and we are eating them in the Park together, me, Debbie who is fifteen, and Jeff who is sixteen. Debbie and Jeff ran away twelve days ago, walked out of school one morning with $100 between them. Because a missing-juvenile is out on Debbie—she was on probation because her mother had once taken her to the police station and declared her incorrigible—this is only the second time they have been out of a friend's apartment since they got to San Francisco. The first time they went over to the Fairmont Hotel and rode the outside elevator, three times up and three times down. "Wow," Jeff says, and that is all he can think to say, about that.

I ask why they ran away.

"My parents said I had to go to church," Debbie says. "And they

wouldn't let me dress the way I wanted. In the seventh grade my skirts were longer than anybody's—it got better in the eighth grade, but still."

"Your mother was kind of a bummer," Jeff agrees.

"They didn't like Jeff. They didn't like my girlfriends. My father thought I was cheap and he told me so. I had a C average and he told me I couldn't date until I raised it, and that bugged me too."

"My mother was just a genuine all-American bitch," Jeff says. "She was really troublesome about hair. Also she didn't like boots. It was really weird."

"Tell about the chores," Debbie says.

"For example I had chores. If I didn't finish ironing my shirts for the week I couldn't go out for the weekend. It was weird. Wow."

Debbie giggles and shakes her head. "This year's gonna be wild."

"We're just gonna let it all happen," Jeff says. "Everything's in the future, you can't pre-plan it. First we get jobs, then a place to live. Then, I dunno."

Jeff finishes off the French fries and gives some thought to what kind of job he could get. "I always kinda dug metal shop, welding, stuff like that." Maybe he could work on cars, I say. "I'm not too mechanically minded," he says. "Anyway you can't pre-plan."

"I could get a job baby-sitting," Debbie says. "Or in a dime store."

"You're always talking about getting a job in a dime store," Jeff says.

"That's because I worked in a dime store already."

Debbie is buffing her fingernails with the belt to her suède jacket. She is annoyed because she chipped a nail and because I do not have any polish remover in the car. I promise to get her to a friend's apartment so that she can redo her manicure, but something has been bothering me and as I fiddle with the ignition I finally ask it. I ask them to think back to when they were children, to tell me what they had wanted to be when they were grown up, how they had seen the future then.

Jeff throws a Coca-Cola bottle out the car window. "I can't remember I ever thought about it," he says.

"I remember I wanted to be a veterinarian once," Debbie says. "But now I'm more or less working in the vein of being an artist or a model or a cosmetologist. Or something."

I hear quite a bit about one cop, Officer Arthur Gerrans, whose name has become a synonym for zealotry on the Street. "He's our Officer Krupke," Max once told me. Max is not personally wild about Officer Gerrans because Officer Gerrans took Max in after the Human Be-In last winter, that's the big Human Be-In in Golden Gate Park where 10,000 people got turned on free, or 10,000 did, or some number did, but then Officer Gerrans has busted almost everyone in the District at one time or another. Presumably to forestall a cult of personality, Officer Gerrans was transferred out of the District not long ago, and when I see him it is not at the Park Station but at the Central Station on Greenwich Avenue.

We are in an interrogation room, and I am interrogating Officer Gerrans. He is young and blond and wary and I go in slow. I wonder what he thinks "the major problems" in the Haight are.

Officer Gerrans thinks it over. "I would say the major problems there," he says finally, "the major problems are narcotics and juveniles. Juveniles and narcotics, those are your major problems."

I write that down.

"Just one moment," Officer Gerrans says, and leaves the room. When he comes back he tells me that I cannot talk to him without permission from Chief Thomas Cahill.

"In the meantime," Officer Gerrans adds, pointing at the notebook in which I have written *major problems: juveniles, narcotics*, "I'll take those notes."

The next day I apply for permission to talk to Officer Gerrans and also to Chief Cahill. A few days later a sergeant returns my call.

"We have finally received clearance from the Chief per your request," the sergeant says, "and that is taboo."

I wonder why it is taboo to talk to Officer Gerrans.

Officer Gerrans is involved in court cases coming to trial.

I wonder why it is taboo to talk to Chief Cahill.

The Chief has pressing police business.

I wonder if I can talk to anyone at all in the Police Department.

"No," the sergeant says, "not at the particular moment."

Which was my last official contact with the San Francisco Police Department.

Norris and I are standing around the Panhandle and Norris is telling me how it is all set up for a friend to take me to Big Sur. I say what I really want to do is spend a few days with Norris and his wife and the rest of the people in their house. Norris says it would be a lot easier if I'd take some acid. I say I'm unstable. Norris says all right, anyway, *grass*, and he squeezes my hand.

One day Norris asks how old I am. I tell him I am thirty-two.

It takes a few minutes, but Norris rises to it. "Don't worry," he says at last. "There's old hippies too."

It is a pretty nice evening and nothing much happened and Max brings his old lady, Sharon, over to the Warehouse. The Warehouse, which is where Don and a floating number of other people live, is not actually a warehouse but the garage of a condemned hotel. The Warehouse was conceived as total theater, a continual happening, and I always feel good there. What happened ten minutes ago or what is going to happen a half hour from now tends to fade from mind at the Warehouse. Somebody is usually doing something interesting, like working on a light show, and there are a lot of interesting things around, like an old Chevrolet touring car which is used as a bed and a vast American flag fluttering up in the shadows and an overstuffed chair suspended like a swing from the rafters, the point of that being that it gives you a sensory-deprivation high.

One reason I particularly like the Warehouse is that a child named Michael is staying there now. Michael's mother, Sue Ann, is a sweet wan girl who is always in the kitchen cooking seaweed or baking macrobiotic bread while Michael amuses himself with joss sticks or an old tambourine or a rocking horse with the paint worn off. The first time I ever saw Michael was on that rocking horse, a very blond and pale and dirty child on a rocking horse with no paint. A blue theatrical spotlight was the only light in the house that afternoon, and there was Michael in it, crooning to the wooden horse. Michael is three years old. He is a bright child but does not yet talk.

This particular night Michael is trying to light his joss sticks and there are the usual number of people floating through and they all drift into Don's room and sit on the bed and pass joints. Sharon is very excited when she arrives. "Don," she cries, breathless. "We got some STP today." At this time STP is a pretty big deal, remember; nobody yet knew what it was and it was relatively, although just relatively, hard to come by. Sharon is blond and scrubbed and probably seventeen, but Max is a little vague about that since his court case comes up in a month or so and he doesn't need statutory rape on top of it. Sharon's parents were living apart when last she saw them. She does not miss school or anything much about her past, except her younger brother. "I want to turn him on," she confided one day. "He's fourteen now, that's the perfect age. I know where he goes to high school and someday I'll just go get him."

Time passes and I lose the thread and when I pick it up again Max seems to be talking about what a beautiful thing it is the way Sharon washes dishes.

"Well it *is* beautiful," Sharon says. "*Every*thing is. I mean you watch that blue detergent blob run on the plate, watch the grease cut—well, it can be a real trip."

Pretty soon now, maybe next month, maybe later, Max and Sharon plan to leave for Africa and India, where they can live off the land. "I got this little trust fund, see," Max says, "which is useful in that it tells cops and border patrols I'm O.K., but living off the land is the thing. You can get your high and get your dope in the city, O.K., but we gotta get out somewhere and live organically."

THE FIRST TIME I EVER SAW MICHAEL WAS ON THAT ROCKING HORSE, A VERY BLOND AND PALE AND DIRTY CHILD ON A ROCKING HORSE WITH NO PAINT.

"Roots and things," Sharon says, lighting another joss stick for Michael. Michael's mother is still in the kitchen cooking seaweed. "You can eat them."

Maybe eleven o'clock, we move from the Warehouse to the place where Max and Sharon live with a couple named Tom and Barbara. Sharon is pleased to get home ["I hope you got some hash joints fixed in the kitchen," she says to Barbara by way of greeting] and everybody is pleased to show off the apartment, which has a lot of flowers and candles and paisleys. Max and Sharon and Tom and Barbara get pretty high on hash, and everyone dances a little and we do some liquid projections and set up a strobe and take turns getting a high on that. Quite late, somebody called Steve comes in with a pretty, dark girl. They have been to a meeting of people who practice a Western yoga, but they do not seem to want to talk about that. They lie on the floor awhile, and then Steve stands up.

"Max," he says, "I want to say one thing."

"It's your trip." Max is edgy.

"I found love on acid. But I lost it. And now I'm finding it again. With nothing but grass."

Max mutters that heaven and hell are both in one's karma.

"That's what bugs me about psychedelic art," Steve says.

"What about psychedelic art," Max says. "I haven't seen much psychedelic art."

Max is lying on a bed with Sharon, and Steve leans down to him. "Groove, baby," he says. "You're a groove."

Steve sits down then and tells me about one summer when he was at a school of design in Rhode Island and took thirty trips, the last ones all bad. I ask why they were bad. "I could tell you it was my neuroses," he says, "but fuck that."

A few days later I drop by to see Steve in his apartment. He paces nervously around the room he uses as a studio and shows me some paintings. We do not seem to be getting to the point.

"Maybe you noticed something going on at Max's," he says abruptly.

It seems that the girl he brought, the dark pretty one, had once been Max's girl. She had followed him to Tangier and now to San Francisco. But Max has Sharon. "So she's kind of staying around here," Steve says.

Steve is troubled by a lot of things. He is twenty-three, was raised in Virginia, and has the idea that California is the beginning of the end. "I feel it's insane," he says, and his voice drops. "This chick tells me there's no meaning to life but it doesn't matter, we'll just flow right out. There've been times I felt like packing up and taking off for the East Coast again, at least there I had a *target*. At least there you expect that it's going to happen." He lights a cigarette for me and his hands shake. "Here you know it's not going to."

I ask what it is that is supposed to happen.

"I don't know," he says. "Something. Anything."

Arthur Lisch is on the telephone in his kitchen, trying to sell VISTA a program for the District. "We already *got* an emergency," he says into the telephone, meanwhile trying to disentangle his daughter, age one and a half, from the cord. "We don't get help, nobody can guarantee what's going to happen. We've got people sleeping in the streets here. We've got people starving to death." He pauses. "All right," he says then, and his voice rises. "So they're doing it by choice. So what."

By the time he hangs up he has limned what strikes me as a Dickensian picture of life on the edge of Golden Gate Park, but then this is my first exposure to Arthur Lisch's "riot-on-the-street-unless" pitch. Arthur Lisch is a kind of leader of the Diggers, who, in the official District mythology, are supposed to be a group of anonymous good guys with no thought in their collective head but to lend a helping hand. The official District mythology also has it that the Diggers have no "leaders," but nonetheless Arthur Lisch is one. Arthur Lisch is also a paid worker for the American Friends' Service Committee and he lives with his wife, Jane, and their two small children in a railroad flat, which on this particular day lacks organization. For one thing the telephone keeps ringing. Arthur promises to attend a hearing at city hall. Arthur promises to "send Edward, he's O.K." Arthur promises to get a good group, maybe the Loading Zone, to play free for a Jewish benefit. For a second thing the baby is crying, and she does not stop until Jane Lisch appears with a jar of Gerber's Junior Chicken Noodle Dinner. Another confusing element is somebody named Bob, who just sits in the room and looks at his toes. First he looks at the toes on one foot, then at the toes on the other. I make several attempts to include Bob in the conversation before I realize he is on a bad trip. Moreover, there are two people hacking up what looks like a side of beef on the kitchen floor, the idea being that when it gets hacked up, Jane Lisch can cook it for the daily Digger feed in the Park.

Arthur Lisch does not seem to notice any of this. He just keeps talking about cybernated societies and the guaranteed annual wage and riot on the Street, unless.

I call the Lisches a day or so later and ask for Arthur. Jane Lisch says he's next door taking a shower because somebody is coming down from a bad trip in their bathroom. Besides the freak-out in the bathroom they are expecting a psychiatrist in to look at Bob. Also a doctor for Edward, who is not O.K. at all but has the flu. Jane says maybe I should talk to Chester Anderson. She will not give me his number.

Chester Anderson is a legacy of the Beat Generation, a man in his middle thirties whose peculiar hold on the District derives from his possession of a mimeograph machine, on which he prints communiqués signed "the communication company." It is another tenet of the official District mythology that the communication company will print anything anybody has to say, but in fact Chester Anderson prints only what he writes himself, agrees with, or considers harmless or dead matter. His statements, which are left in piles and pasted on windows around Haight Street, are regarded with some apprehension in the District and with considerable interest by outsiders, who study them, like China watchers, for subtle shifts in obscure ideologies. An

Anderson communiqué might be doing something as specific as fingering someone who is said to have set up a marijuana bust, or it might be working in a more general vein:

> Pretty little 16-year-old middle-class chick comes to the Haight to see what it's all about & gets picked up by a 17-year-old street dealer who spends all day shooting her full of speed again & again, then feeds her 3,000 mikes & raffles off her temporarily unemployed body for the biggest Haight Street gangbang since the night before last. The politics and ethics of ecstasy. Rape is as common as bullshit on Haight Street. Kids are starving on the Street. Minds and bodies are being maimed as we watch, a scale model of Vietnam.

Somebody other than Jane Lisch gave me an address for Chester Anderson, 443 Arguello, but 443 Arguello does not exist. I telephone the wife of the man who gave me 443 Arguello and she says it's 742 Arguello.

"But don't go up there," she says.

I say I'll telephone.

"There's no number," she says. "I can't give it to you."

"742 Arguello," I say.

"No," she says. "I don't know. And don't go there. And don't use either my name or my husband's name if you do."

She is the wife of a full professor of English at San Francisco State College. I decide to lie low on the question of Chester Anderson for awhile.

> *Paranoia strikes deep—*
> *Into your life it will creep—*
>   is a song the Buffalo
>   Springfield sings.

The appeal of Malakoff Diggings has kind of faded out but Max says why don't I come to his place, just be there, the next time he takes acid. Tom will take it too, probably Sharon, maybe Barbara. We can't do it for six or seven days because Max and Tom are in STP space now. They are not crazy about STP but it has advantages. "You've still got your forebrain," Tom says. "I could write behind STP, but not behind acid."

This is the first time I have heard of anything you can't do behind acid, also the first time I have heard that Tom writes.

Otto is feeling better because he discovered it wasn't the cocaine-and-wheat that made him sick. It was the chicken pox, which he caught baby-sitting for Big Brother and the Holding Company one night when they were playing. I go over to see him and meet Vicki, who sings now and then with a group called the Jook Savages and lives at Otto's place. Vicki dropped out of Laguna High "because I had mono," followed the Grateful Dead up to San Francisco one time and has been here "for a while." Her mother and father are divorced, and she does not see her father, who works for a network in New York. A few months ago he came out to do a documentary on the District and tried to find her, but couldn't. Later he wrote her a letter in care of her mother urging her to go back to school. Vicki guesses maybe she will sometime but she doesn't see much point in it right now

We are eating a little tempura in Japantown, Chet Helms and I, and he is sharing some of his insights with me. Until a couple of years ago Chet Helms never did much besides hitchhiking, but now he runs the Avalon Ballroom and flies over the Pole to check out the London scene and says things like "Just for the sake of clarity I'd like to categorize the aspects of primitive religion as I see it." Right now he is talking about Marshall McLuhan and how the printed word is finished, out, over. "*The East Village Other* is one of the few papers in America whose books are in the black," he says. "I know that from reading *Barron's*."

> **THE BIG STROBE WAS GOING AND THE COLORED LIGHTS AND THE DAY-GLO PAINTING AND THE PLACE WAS FULL OF HIGH-SCHOOL KIDS TRYING TO LOOK TURNED ON.**

A new group is supposed to play in the Panhandle today but they are having trouble with the amplifier and I sit in the sun listening to a couple of little girls, maybe seventeen years old. One of them has a lot of makeup and the other wears Levi's and cowboy boots. The boots do not look like an affectation, they look like she came up off a ranch about two weeks ago. I wonder what she is doing here in the Panhandle trying to make friends with a city girl who is snubbing her but I do not wonder long, because she is homely and awkward and I think of her going all the way through the consolidated union high school out there where she comes from and nobody ever asking her to go into Reno on Saturday night for a drive-in movie and a beer on the riverbank, so she runs. "I know a thing about dollar bills," she is saying now. "You get one that says 'IIII' in one corner and 'IIII' in another, you take it down to Dallas, Texas, they'll give you $15 for it."

"Who will?" the city girl asks.

"I don't know."

"There are only three significant pieces of data in the world today," is another thing Chet Helms told me one night. We were at the Avalon and the big strobe was going and the colored lights and the Day-Glo painting and the place was full of high-school kids trying to look turned on. The Avalon sound system projects 126 decibels at 100 feet but to Chet Helms the sound is just there, like the air, and he talks through it. "The first is," he said, "God died last year and was obited by the press. The second is, fifty percent of the population is or will be under twenty-five." A boy shook a tambourine toward us and Chet smiled benevolently at him. "The third," he said, "is that they got twenty billion irresponsible dollars to spend."

Thursday comes, some Thursday, and Max and Tom and Sharon and maybe Barbara are going to take some acid. They want to drop it about three o'clock. Barbara has baked fresh bread, Max has gone to the Park for fresh flowers, and Sharon is making a sign for the door which reads "DO NOT DISTURB, RING, KNOCK, OR IN ANY OTHER WAY DISTURB. LOVE." This is not how I would put it to either the health inspector, who is due this week, or any of the several score narcotics agents in the neighborhood, but I figure the sign is Sharon's trip.

Once the sign is finished Sharon gets restless. "Can I at least play the new record?" she asks Max.

"Tom and Barbara want to save it for when we're high."

"I'm getting bored, just sitting around here."

Max watches her jump up and walk out. "That's what you call pre-acid uptight jitters," he says.

Barbara is not in evidence. Tom keeps walking in and out. "All these innumerable last-minute things you have to do," he mutters.

"It's a tricky thing, acid," Max says after a while. He is turning the stereo on and off. "When a chick takes acid, it's all right if she's alone, but when she's living with somebody this edginess comes out.

And if the hour-and-a-half process before you take the acid doesn't go smooth . . . " He picks up a roach and studies it, then adds, "They're having a little thing back there with Barbara."

Sharon and Tom walk in.

"You pissed off too?" Max asks Sharon.

Sharon does not answer.

Max turns to Tom. "Is she all right?"

"Yeh."

"Can we take acid?" Max is on edge.

"I don't know what she's going to do."

"What do you want to do?"

"What I want to do depends on what she wants to do." Tom is rolling some joints, first rubbing the papers with a marijuana resin he makes himself. He takes the joints back to the bedroom, and Sharon goes with him.

"Something like this happens every time people take acid," Max says. After a while he brightens and develops a theory around it. "Some people don't like to go out of themselves, that's the trouble. You probably wouldn't. You'd probably like only a quarter of a tab. There's still an ego on a quarter tab, and it wants things. Now if that thing is balling—and your old lady or your old man is off somewhere flashing and doesn't want to be touched—well, you get put down on acid, you can be on a bummer for months."

Sharon drifts in, smiling. "Barbara might take some acid, we're all feeling better, we smoked a joint."

At three-thirty that afternoon Max, Tom, and Sharon placed tabs under their tongues and sat down together in the living room to wait for the flash. Barbara stayed in the bedroom, smoking hash. During the next four hours a window banged once in Barbara's room, and about five-thirty some children had a fight on the street. A curtain billowed in the afternoon wind. A cat scratched a beagle in Sharon's lap. Except for the sitar music on the stereo there was no other sound or movement until seven-thirty, when Max said "Wow."

I spot Deadeye on Haight Street, and he gets in the car. Until we get off the Street he sits very low and inconspicuous. Deadeye wants me to meet his old lady, but first he wants to talk to me about how he got hip to helping people.

"Here I was, just a tough kid on a motorcycle," he says, "and suddenly I see that young people don't have to walk alone." Deadeye has a clear evangelistic gaze and the reasonable rhetoric of a car salesman. He is society's model product. I try to meet his gaze directly because he once told me he could read character in people's eyes, particularly if he has just dropped acid, which he did, about nine o'clock this morning. "They just have to remember one thing," he says. "The Lord's Prayer. And that can help them in more ways than one."

He takes a much-folded letter from his wallet. The letter is from a little girl he helped. "My loving brother," it begins. "I thought I'd write you a letter since I'm a part of you. Remember that: When you feel happiness, I do, when you feel…"

> **"BASICALLY I'M A POET," SHE SAYS, "BUT I HAD MY GUITAR STOLEN JUST AFTER I ARRIVED AND THAT KIND OF HUNG UP MY THING."**

"What I want to do now," Deadeye says, "is set up a house where a person of any age can come, spend a few days, talk over his problems. *Any age.* People your age, they've got problems too."

I say a house will take money.

"I've found a way to make money," Deadeye says. He hesitates only a few seconds. "I could've made eighty-five dollars on the Street just then. See, in my pocket I had a hundred tabs of acid. I had to come up with twenty dollars by tonight or we're out of the house we're in, so I knew somebody who had acid, and I knew somebody who wanted it, so I made the connection."

Since the Mafia moved into the LSD racket, the quantity is up and the quality is down… Historian Arnold Toynbee celebrated his 78th birthday Friday night by snapping his fingers and tapping his toes to the Quicksilver Messenger Service… are a couple of items from Herb Caen's column one morning as the West declined in the spring of 1967.

When I was in San Francisco a tab, or a cap, of LSD-25 sold for three to five dollars, depending upon the seller and the district. LSD was slightly cheaper in the Haight-Ashbury than in the Fillmore, where it was used rarely, mainly as a sexual ploy, and sold by pushers of hard drugs, *e.g.*, heroin, or "smack." A great deal of acid was being cut with Methedrine, which is the trade name for an amphetamine, because Methedrine can simulate the flash that low-quality acid lacks. Nobody knows how much LSD is actually in a tab, but the standard trip is supposed to be 250 micrograms. Grass was running ten dollars a lid, five dollars a matchbox. Hash was considered "a luxury item." All the amphetamines, or "speed"—Benzedrine, Dexedrine, and particularly Methedrine—were in far more common use in the late spring than they had been in the early spring. Some attributed this to the presence of the Syndicate; others to a general deterioration of the scene, to the incursions of gangs and younger part-time, or "plastic," hippies, who like the amphetamines and the illusions of action and power they give. Where Methedrine is in wide use, heroin tends to be available, because, I was told, "You can get awful damn high shooting crystal, and smack can be used to bring you down."

Deadeye's old lady, Gerry, meets us at the door of their place. She is a big, hearty girl who has always counseled at Girl Scout camps during summer vacations and was "in social welfare" at the University of Washington when she decided that she "just hadn't done enough living" and came to San Francisco. "Actually the heat was bad in Seattle," she adds.

"The first night I got down here," she says, "I stayed with a gal I met over at the Blue Unicorn. I looked like I'd just arrived, had a knapsack and stuff." After that, Gerry stayed at a house the Diggers were running, where she met Deadeye. "Then it took time to get my bearings, so I haven't done much work yet."

I ask Gerry what work she does. "Basically I'm a poet," she says, "but I had my guitar stolen right after I arrived, and that kind of hung up my thing."

"Get your books," Deadeye orders. "Show her your books." Gerry demurs, then goes into the bedroom and comes back with several theme books full of verse. I leaf through them but Deadeye is still talking about helping people. "Any kid that's on speed," he says, "I'll try to get him off it. The only advantage to it from the kids' point of view is that you don't have to worry about sleeping or eating."

"Or sex," Gerry adds.

"That's right. When you're strung out on crystal you don't need *nothing*."

"It can lead to the hard stuff," Gerry says. "Take your average Meth freak, once he's started putting the needle in his arm, it's not too hard to say, well, let's shoot a little smack."

All the while I am looking at Gerry's poems. They are a very young girl's poems, each written out in a neat hand and finished off with a curlicue. Dawns are roseate, skies silver-tinted. When Gerry writes "crystal" in her books, she does not mean Meth.

"You gotta get back to your writing," Deadeye says fondly, but Gerry ignores this. She is telling about somebody who propositioned her yesterday. "He just walked up to me on the Street, offered me six hundred dollars to go to Reno and do the thing."

"You're not the only one he approached," Deadeye says.

"If some chick wants to go with him, fine," Gerry says. "Just don't bum my trip." She empties the tuna-fish can we are using for an ashtray and goes over to look at a girl who is asleep on the floor. It is the same girl who was sleeping on the floor the first day I came to Deadeye's place. She has been sick a week now, ten days. "Usually when somebody comes up to me on the Street like that," Gerry adds, "I hit him for some change."

When I saw Gerry in the Park the next day I asked her about the sick girl, and Gerry said cheerfully that she was in the hospital, with pneumonia.

JOAN DIDION's iconic essay, "Slouching Towards Bethlehem," (excerpted here) first appeared in *The Saturday Evening Post* on September 23, 1967. The stark reporting of San Francisco's Haight-Ashbury community received widespread praise from critics. The piece anchored her collection of essays about California life and the 1960s, published by Farrar, Straus & Giroux in 1968.

INDEX

INDEX

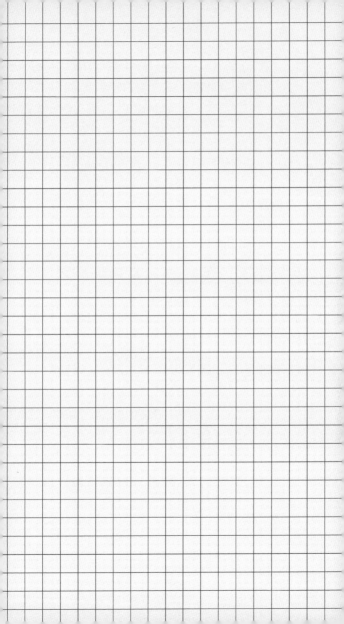